PAPER FOLDING TEMPLATES
FOR PRINT DESIGN

PAPER FOLDING
TEMPLATES
FOR PRINT DESIGN

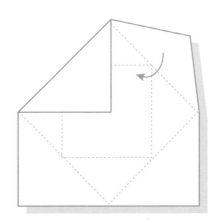

FORMATS, TECHNIQUES, AND DESIGN CONSIDERATIONS
FOR INNOVATIVE PAPER FOLDING

TRISH WITKOWSKI

For more excellent books and resources for designers,
visit **www.howdesign.com**.

14 13 12 11 10   5 4 3 2 1

Distributed in Canada by Fraser Direct
100 Armstrong Avenue
Georgetown, Ontario, Canada L7G 5S4
Tel: (905) 877-4411

Library of Congress Cataloging-in-Publication Data

ISBN 10: 1440314128
ISBN 13: 9781440314124

Commissioning Editor: Isheeta Mustafi
Design concept: Draft Associates
Layout: Tony Seddon
Art Director: Emily Portnoi
Photography: Jason Edwards

CONTENTS

INTRODUCTION

There are many, many ways to fold a sheet of paper, but looking at the mail and all the other folded print materials we are exposed to every day, one might think that paper folding for print production has some serious limitations.

Not true. As a matter of fact, folding is quite possibly the most varied and creative of ways to alter the presentation and experience of printed materials—but who would know? After all, how many folding styles can you name? The good news is that you do not have to know about every folding style in existence to create stylish and compelling folded print materials. You just need a general understanding of the folding families and their characteristics, as this will help you to start ruling in and ruling out different categories of folding. You will also need basic knowledge of finishing processes

such as folding, scoring, die-cutting, and trimming. This will aid in the creative and production processes, as understanding how and where you can take advantage of the capabilities of the print medium can only help the process. And then, of course, you need some great examples of folded materials to look at—so having a book like this to refer to helps a lot as well!

CREATIVITY AT ANY BUDGET

When it comes to designing for printed materials, most people tend to fall in one of two categories—high budget or low-to-moderate budget. Those on a fairly conservative budget often feel as though their hands are tied and that their creative folding options are limited. This group tends to fold on auto-pilot, choosing from two or three "go-to" folding

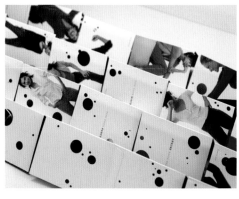

Hexagon-shaped Iron-Cross Fold by Texas State University **(above)** *Two-way Circular Gate fold by Whitmore Group and J Kozak Creative* **(top right)** *Meandering Accordion by Design Ranch* **(bottom right)**

styles for every project. The high-budget folks are under a lot of pressure to be creative, but they do not know what exciting folding options are available to them, which makes what should be a fascinating process stressful and overwhelming instead.

This book is designed to address both categories, offering inexpensive ways to spice up the everyday, with fresh tips and tricks that will surprise you, and a whole section devoted to interesting low- to moderate-budget folded solutions. There is also an entire section that focuses on unusual and creative folded solutions that are great for that special, higher-budget project. There is something for everybody, so enjoy.

Oblong-format Roll Fold with arrow die-cut cover by Neenah Paper **(top left)** . *Angled direct mailpiece by Suttle Straus* **(left)** *Vertical-format Wrapped Stepped Accordion by Chartreuse and Oliver Printing Co* **(above)**

USING THIS BOOK

This book was created to serve as a springboard for creativity, as a conversation starter, and as a technical resource for digital file creation. For best results, enlist the help of a print professional at the earliest stages of the process to assist with planning the production of your project, and to check the plan against the budget.

For those who plan to create their own production file or modify the overall configuration of any of the featured folds, diagrams are included to offer information regarding proper file setup. Please note that there are two diagrams for each—side one and side two of the digital document. The diagram is meant to be used as a guideline for discussion with a print production professional, and may be modified after all project variables have been considered.

At the back of this book is a CD that contains ready-to-use blank digital templates of the folds featured in chapters three and four of this book. Die-lines are created to trim size, so bleeds must be pulled past the document edge. It is strongly recommended to keep the fold guides and fold marks locked on their layers, and to ensure that any resizing or technical modifications to the templates are done cautiously or with the help of a print production professional.

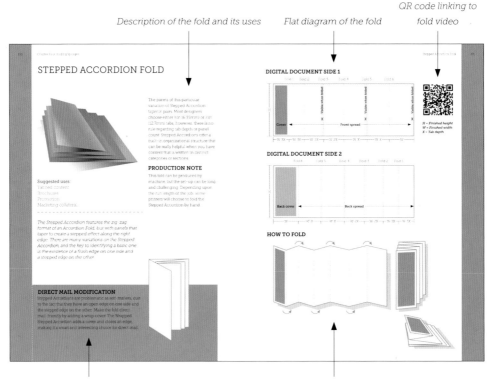

Description of the fold and its uses   *Flat diagram of the fold*   *QR code linking to fold video*

Tips and modifications   *Folding instructions*

COMMUNICATING FOLDING INTENT—
THE RIGHT WAY

When sending a laser mock-up to the printer, send a folding sequence dummy to ensure proper folding intent is communicated. All it takes is a moment and a pen.

To get started:

Make a folded laser mock-up, paying close attention to how it folds. Then lay it out flat, concentrating on the first fold. What needs to be communicated to the printer is which panels will meet (or kiss), and in what order. To do this is simple. Using the Roll-Fold as an example, locate the first fold and draw a line connecting the two panels and label each panel "A" or "1" (see 1a). Fold those two panels together and see which two panels will meet next. Again, draw the line visually connecting the two panels and then label them each "B" or "2" (see 1b). Continue to do this for the remainder of the folds until the piece is completely folded. When the piece is laid out flat again, the lines and letters may look odd, but this is how printers communicate, and the markings make it nearly impossible to confuse folding intent.

TIP

Don't get intimidated by a specialty fold. This book features many "exotic" folding options, and depending upon your project quantity, you may be surprised at how affordable a specialty solution can be. For example, if the quantity is high enough (over 10,000), there are binderies with special capabilities that may be able to machine-fold your piece. If the quantity is low (in the hundreds to a few thousand), hand-folding likely won't break the bank. It always pays to do a little research before ruling out a solution.

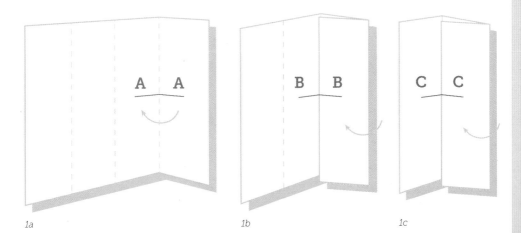

1a   1b   1c

CHAPTER ONE: THE BASICS

Before pushing the medium of folding for print design, it's important to understand the process itself, the language and the nuances between different styles of folding and their general characteristics. Knowledge of this material will help you to better communicate with your print service providers, and will also give you a good feel for what your options are and how you can use different types of folding techniques to maximize the value of your print projects.

Choosing the right folding style for your project is one component of the design process, however. There are several other decisions that must be made as well—including which paper to choose, whether or not to utilize scoring, whether to print digitally or conventionally, and even where to place critical marketing messages in the folded layout. The delivery method also comes into play at this point in the process as well, given that there are many format-related considerations for pieces that must go through the mailstream.

So, even though this chapter is called The Basics, don't be tempted to skip it. This information is critically important in your foundation knowledge about folding.

Why fold?

• Folding is a great way to get a lot of information into a compact size.

• Each folding style has a distinct order of opening. You can use folding as a way to lead the recipient through the material.

• Folding can be creative and distinctive, or simple and straightforward.

• Folding is dimensional. It's always a surprise, as you never can tell exactly what fold you will get until the piece is opened.

• Folding can help you organize information so that it presents logically and in the right order.

Not just a niche

There is a common misconception in the graphic arts industry that there is only so much that can be done with folding for print. Many see practical folding as a limited handful of standard styles, and anything interesting is assumed to be unattainable. This book offers creativity for both low and high budgets, and will prove that practical folding is almost limitless in its possibilities.

FOLDING FAMILIES

All folded materials have distinct characteristics that allow them to be classified into folding families. Knowing a bit about the different families will help you to understand your options when you begin thinking about a project, and will help you rule in/rule out different categories of folds based on your concept, content, and project specifications.

To be able to properly identify brochure folds, it is important to understand what to look for—such as what characteristics make a Roll Fold different from a Gate Fold, etc. There are eight folding families: Accordions, Basics, Exotics, Gates, Maps, Parallels, Posters, and Rolls.

Closed Gate Fold by Keystone Resources

THE FOLDING FAMILIES
The icons below illustrate the unique identifying characteristics of each folding family.

Accordion Folds

Map Folds

Basic Folds

Parallel Folds

Exotic Folds

Poster Folds

Gate Folds

Roll Folds

ACCORDIONS

Accordion Folds are some of the most common styles used in brochure folding. The common characteristic of Accordion Folds is the "zig-zag" back-and-forth nature of the panels. Accordions are broad in their variations and are an excellent choice for a variety of applications.

Stepped Accordion

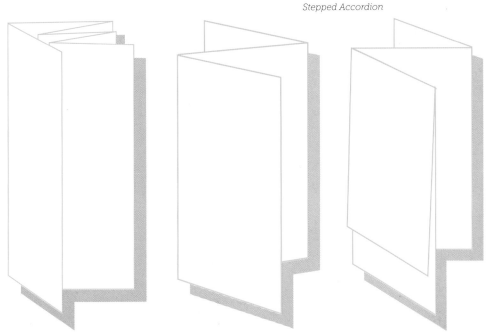

Wrapped Accordion

Standard Accordion

Accordion with outside short fold

BASICS

The Basic folding family consists of some of the easiest and most common folding styles. Great for low budget or simple projects, these styles are perfect for invitations, newsletters, and brochures, and virtually guarantee stress-free production at almost any printer or bindery.

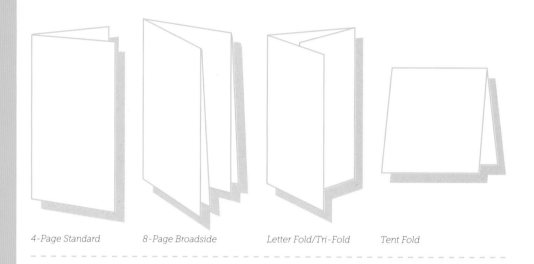

4-Page Standard　　　*8-Page Broadside*　　　*Letter Fold/Tri-Fold*　　　*Tent Fold*

EXOTICS

The Exotic family is the most exciting of the bunch. Filled with unrelated Specialty Folds that challenge even the most creative mind, many of these styles require either the services of a specialty bindery, or hand-folding. Exotics can include unique shapes, diagonal folds, and unusual formats.

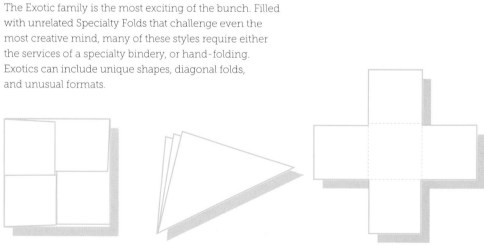

Box Top　　　　　　*Triangle Fold*　　　　　　*Iron Cross Fold*

GATES

Gate Folds are generally symmetrical, with two or more panels folding into the center from opposing sides. Gate Folds often require the addition of a knife folder, gate fold attachment, or plow folder to execute (or hand-folding to finish). Gate Folds offer a nice "reveal" and work well for direct mail and brochures.

Gate Fold

Open Gate

Closed Gate

Double Gate

MAPS

Map Folds characteristically have several Accordion Folds and are built in a tall format that opens into a large continuous layout, rather than spreads. Maps are limited to lighter-weight stocks and may require special machinery configurations.

3-Story Map

4-Story Map

2-Story Map

PARALLELS

The Parallel folding family consists of styles with panels that stay parallel to each other. Parallel Folds run the gamut from simple to complicated, and offer a variety of options suitable for almost any application.

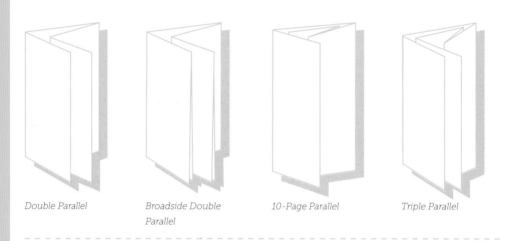

Double Parallel   *Broadside Double Parallel*   *10-Page Parallel*   *Triple Parallel*

POSTERS

Poster Folds are combination folds that are built to open out into a large poster format. Posters consist of at least two folds: one serves as the base fold, and one as the finished fold. The base fold is the first folding style applied; the finished fold is the folding style it adapts for the finished format. Posters are limited to lighter-weight stocks.

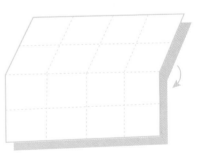

Double Parallel into Accordion Poster Fold. Step 1.

Step 2

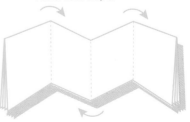

Step 3

ROLLS

Roll Folds consist of four or more panels that roll in
on each other. The roll-in panels must get incrementally
smaller to be able to tuck into the respective panels,
which makes file set-up for the Roll Fold very tricky. Roll
Folds are nice for brochures and marketing materials;
however they are not great for large bodies of copy,
since reading order can be confused as the viewer
rolls open the panels.

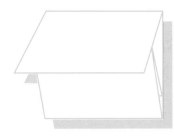

Vertical Roll

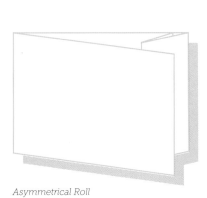

Asymmetrical Roll

Roll Fold

Reverse Roll

- -

Proprietary and branded solutions

There is an additional category of folds that tend to fall
under the Exotic family, but that must be singled out for
their status. There are companies that have developed
unique solutions and patented or branded them. The
patented solutions are called "proprietary solutions" and
the folded solutions that are not patented and have been
marketed under a trademarked name are considered
"branded solutions." If the solution is owned, in many
cases you must work with the patent holder to be able to
use that fold for your project. Most Exotic (Specialty) folds
are not patented. Simply look for a patent number and
company credit on the folded piece to be sure, and
contact the company listed with the number, or look
up the patent number online to learn more.

SPEAKING THE LANGUAGE OF FOLDING

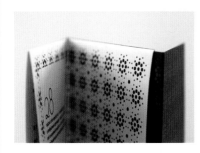

*Tri-Fold with nested 8-page Short Fold
by Kanella Arapoglou*

The language of folding has long been miscommunicated, misinterpreted, and misconstrued. Come to think of it, fold-speak is probably the most casual of all languages in the graphic arts industry. The problem lies in the fact that folding is largely tactile, visual, and dimensional. We are often looking at folded samples, and verbally describing and specifying folded materials—which leaves a lot open to interpretation. Folding terminology, like any terminology passed along verbally for years and years, will evolve and change—sometimes it gets better, and sometimes it just gets confusing.

There is a language of folding that, if mastered, will help you to better communicate with the graphic arts professionals you do business with. Learn these terms and you will drastically reduce the likelihood of having a production problem on your folded projects.

FOLDING COMPENSATION

What looks like a folding mistake by the bindery is often designer error. Paper is dimensional, so if a panel is to fold into another, it must be slightly smaller or there will be what is called "telescoping." Telescoping is the inability of the folded sheet to lie flat. The brochure will have a roundish profile because the panels are too long and push against each other for lack of anywhere else to go.

The bindery will adjust the panels so there is no telescoping, but margins and color breaks will shift noticeably. For best results, adjust for folding compensation in your digital file. If you are unsure of how to do this, consult your printer, or use a professional folding template.

Folding compensation

FLAT SIZE AND FINISHED SIZE

The flat size is the exact dimension of the piece when laid flat. This measurement should include all folding compensations, but should never include bleed allowances because bleed is pulled past the edge of the page in the digital document. Digital document page dimensions and flat size should always be the same measurement. Finished size is the exact dimension of the piece when completely folded.

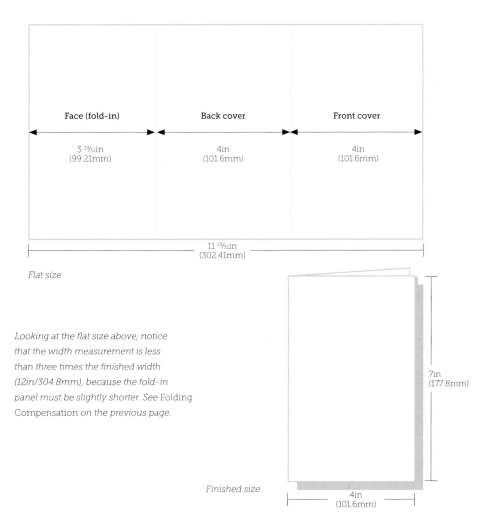

Face (fold-in)	Back cover	Front cover
3 ²⁹⁄₃₂in (99.21mm)	4in (101.6mm)	4in (101.6mm)

11 ²⁹⁄₃₂in (302.41mm)

Flat size

Looking at the flat size above, notice that the width measurement is less than three times the finished width (12in/304.8mm), because the fold-in panel must be slightly shorter. See Folding Compensation *on the previous page.*

7in (177.8mm)

Finished size

4in (101.6mm)

PANELS AND PAGES

Panels are two-sided sections of the final folded piece. A page is one side of a panel. For example, the Accordion Fold below is three panels, each of the three panels is two-sided, and each side is considered a page. So, the Accordion Fold has six pages and three panels. If we take that same fold and make it a Broadside Accordion Fold instead, then it changes to six panels and the page count rises to 12.

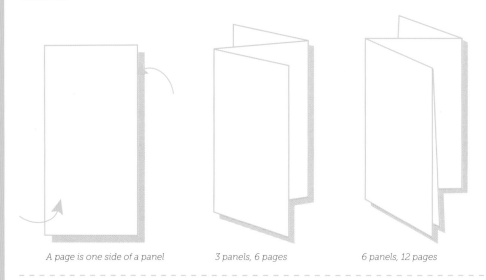

A page is one side of a panel   *3 panels, 6 pages*   *6 panels, 12 pages*

PAGES AND SPREADS

A page is one side of a panel. Spreads are two or more pages meant to be viewed as one. For example, in the Roll Fold, the cover is a page, the back cover is a page, but the inside pages are viewed at the same time when the piece is opened up, and therefore those pages together are considered a spread.

4-page spread

PARALLEL FOLDS AND RIGHT-ANGLE FOLDS

The first fold of any folding style is always a parallel fold. The next fold can be a parallel or a right-angle fold, depending upon the folding style. Parallel folds are parallel to each other. Right-angle folds combine with parallel folds to make right (90°) angles. So, a right-angle fold cannot happen without a parallel fold. Below, a tall-format Double Parallel Fold is finished with a right angle fold. This fold could be described to a printer as "Two parallel folds, one right angle fold."

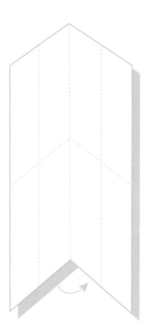

Parallel Fold

Folds stay parallel to each other

Right-angle fold folds at 90˚

BROADSIDE FOLDS, SHORT FOLDS, AND INVERTED SHORT FOLDS

A Broadside Fold doubles its area by folding in half on itself before any characteristic folding style is created. For example, a Broadside Tri-Fold is 12 pages, whereas the tri-fold is six.

A Short Fold is a Broadside Fold, too. The only difference is that the Broadside is a little less than twice the area because in a Short Fold the fold-over panels are shorter than the finished height. How much shorter is a design preference, and the Short Fold can fall to the inside or outside of the brochure. An inverted Short Fold changes direction and pulls downward, offering a variety of creative options.

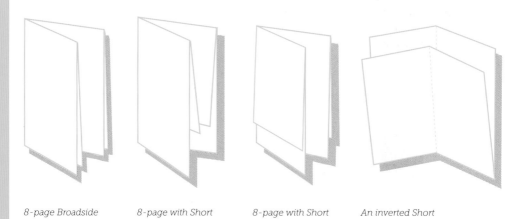

8-page Broadside

8-page with Short Fold to interior

8-page with Short Fold to exterior

An inverted Short Fold pulls downward

AUTOMATION, SEMI-AUTOMATION, AND HAND-FOLDING

Automated-folding, or machine-folding, is when the folded piece is finished entirely by machine for greatest speed and production efficiency. Most of the folds we see in print production today are mechanical folds. Often, due to limitations of equipment, a fold is taken as far as it can go by machine, then the last fold or two is done by hand by workers in the bindery. This is called semi-automation.

Hand-folding is done entirely by hand, but this is not always due to the limitations of machinery. For small quantities, it is sometimes easier to fold the pieces by hand than it is to take the time to set up and use a folding machine. Some folding styles that are normally considered hand-folds can be done by machine at specialty binderies if the quantity is high enough to justify engineering the machinery to execute sophisticated folding configurations. Expensive and quite impractical for extremely long runs, hand-folding requires a die-score and extra time built into the finishing schedule.

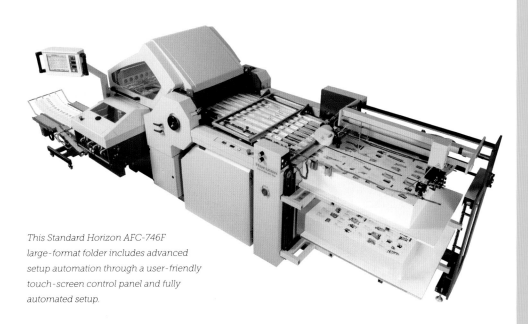

This Standard Horizon AFC-746F large-format folder includes advanced setup automation through a user-friendly touch-screen control panel and fully automated setup.

CHOOSING THE RIGHT PAPER FOR YOUR FOLDED PROJECT

A fabulous fold can be a total flop if it is printed on the wrong paper. You have seen it before—the folded piece that feels wimpy, or the brochure that looks too bulky when it is folded, or worse, weighs too much at the post office. It is a detail that is commonly overlooked, as designers and print buyers often make their judgment call with the pinch of a page in a paper swatchbook.

The best thing to do is to ask your printer or local paper rep for paper dummies in a few different weights, or for a few flat sheets of each choice so that you can whip up your own folded samples. You may be surprised at what you get once the paper is folded down into the desired format. That sheet you were so sure of may no longer even be in the running.

Paper choice affects the character of a piece. The sample above is on an uncoated sheet with die-cutting; the sample below has heavy ink coverage and metallics on a dull coated sheet.

Twist fold by Sappi Fine Paper

Some folding styles require a heavier-weight sheet for stability. This Stepped Accordion/Swinger combo fold is the perfect example. This piece would fail on a lightweight sheet.

STRUCTURE AND SUBSTANCE

Some folding styles are almost sculptural in their format. These folds often make a statement when opened, or can even hold their shape when displayed on a table. Structural folds require the special selection of a heavier sheet because they rely on the stiffness of the sheet to hold their shape. A few examples of folding styles that need a heavier sheet for structural purposes include the Pop-out Accordion, Swinger Fold, and Open Gate.

On the flip side, some folding styles simply cannot be executed on a heavier sheet. Poster folds and folds with multiple or thick right-angle folds (like maps), and book signatures will not work on a heavier sheet. The heavier paper causes problems with air entrapment and unsightly stress-related issues like wrinkles in the corner joints, cracking, and reopening.

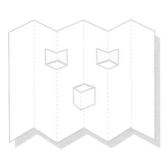

Pop-out Accordion

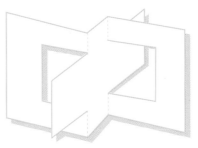

Swinger Fold

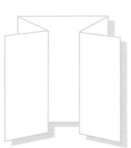

Open Gate

THE TACTILE QUALITY

The greatest thing about paper is its tactile quality.
Weight plays a role in that, but so does finish. Do you
want the hard finish of a high-gloss sheet, or the "toothy"
finish of an uncoated sheet? Your content will present
very differently on these two surfaces, and will send the
recipient subliminal messages about your company
and your brand.

Angled direct mailpiece by Suttle Straus
(left) *Short cover and die-cut by Premier
Press and Sandstrom Partners* **(below)**

STANDING OUT OF THE CROWD

A unique choice of paper can make a folded piece stand out and get noticed. Open the mailbox on an ordinary day and you will usually find a sea of whites, warm whites, blue whites, off-whites—but look, there's a colored envelope! Which will you open first? What about a folded invitation printed on a rich navy blue paper, blind embossed and foil stamped? Sounds like an event worth going to. That same invitation printed two colors on 80lb white paper sets an entirely different level of expectation for the event.

Paper choice makes a big difference—so put some thoughtful consideration into making the final decision. Coated or uncoated? Text or cover weight? Do you choose a colored sheet or a white sheet? If it's white, what shade of white will best represent your content and your client? Feeling overwhelmed? Ask your printer or paper representative for a few paper dummies in selected stocks and weights to evaluate. It can also be helpful to ask your printer if there are any sheets they've had great experience running jobs on recently.

You can mimic the effect of a colored sheet by printing heavy ink coverage on a white sheet. Often this is done to preserve the flesh tones and the highlights in the placed photography, or to create an exact color match that may not exist as a colored sheet. Colored sheets can be highly impactful, but work closely with a printer and/or mailhouse, as you may need to use some special printing techniques (opaque inks, double hits, etc.) to get the best quality result, and there are certain issues with color and contrast that can affect mailability. Planning ahead and starting the conversation early is always the best strategy.

FOLDING AND GRAIN DIRECTION

The way that paper fibers are laid down in sheets during manufacture determines the grain direction.

Hand-made paper

The highly diluted pulp of hand-made paper is evenly spread over a web through manual shaking. This causes the fibers to follow a random orientation, so there is no discernible grain direction in hand-made paper.

Machine-manufactured paper

Paper produced by machine—vat machines or long web machines— has a pronounced grain direction because the fibers align themselves parallel to the direction of movement on the machine.

Depending upon the quality of the paper, folded sheets retain a certain degree of resilience after folding which give them a tendency to reopen. The angle of opening is least with parallel folds, and most noticeable with right-angle folds.

A fold is cleaner and more resilient when the grain is parallel to the fold. A fold against the grain may not lie as flat and can cause cracking, most noticeably in areas of heavy ink coverage. A fold against the grain is also less resilient, and the pressure exerted by the rollers of the folding machine must be somewhat less to avoid an excessive weakening of the paper along the fold line. If folding against the grain is a must, careful paper selection and scoring can alleviate some of these problems.

THE ROLE OF SCORING IN THE FOLDING PROCESS

Scoring uses a mechanical process to compress the paper fibers and decrease stiffness, enabling a high-quality fold. Short of the obvious scoring candidate, such as a heavy sheet or critical fold against the grain, scoring can serve as anything from an aid for hand-finishing, to a guide for critical fold placement, to an insurance policy on a high-budget job.

Remember that brochure you designed with the black cover that had the disappointing white show-through on the fold? That's called cracking. Paper is fiber-based, and the mechanical folding process causes a lot of stress to the sheet, so the fibers and the coating on the sheet can crack and expose an ugly rough texture at the fold. This is most noticeable on a fold against the grain of a heavy sheet—and if there is solid ink coverage across that fold, you will really notice it. Scoring is the best way to alleviate this problem.

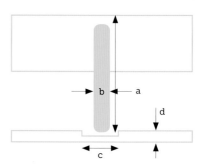

THE MECHANISM OF SCORING

a *Rule height*
b *Rule width*
c *Female die width*
d *Counter height*

V-format Pop-up mailer for Circus (airdate: 2010 on PBS); © PBS 2011; circus piece: design by Christopher Richard; production by Westland Printers

DO I REALLY NEED TO SCORE?

When it comes to scoring, there is often some subjectivity as to whether or not you really need to do it. Although we all like to think we would put the quality of the product first, above all else, the budget sometimes calls for corner-cutting, and scoring is often the first thing to go—clients would rather take a chance and hope for an acceptable result (not too much cracking), than to spend the money to ensure the best quality. But before you jump to conclusions, assuming that scoring is going to bust your budget, know that scoring techniques and technologies have changed a lot over the years. It might be worth checking with your printer to see if they have invested in inline finishing equipment—it is not for every project, but this alternative to offline finishing can be faster and cheaper, and can provide a high-quality result.

If you must use a letterpress score, which is the highest quality and most expensive scoring method, know that all finishing techniques are not necessarily separate "a la carte" items. Scoring, perforating, and die-cutting are all similar processes—creating an impression on the sheet with metal. Because of this, they can often be achieved in the same pass. For example, your printer may be able to make a letterpress die that scores, die-cuts, and perforates all in one impression. Rotary scoring uses a different process, but can also be done simultaneously. So always ask your printer before you decide to skip the cool die-cut window on the cover because you assume you need to pay extra for scoring.

Still on the fence? Do not gamble with quality to save a few bucks. If your printer strongly suggests that the piece should be scored, then listen. They can look at your project and know where the problems will be, so trust their judgment.

SCORING TIPS

Scoring greatly enhances the quality of the fold. However, once the score has been placed, there is no ability for the printer to "tweak" the fold placement, so analyze your proofs very carefully and express your concerns about critical fold placement ahead of time.

You should consider scoring if:
- You are using a sheet that is 100lb text or above
- You are folding against the grain of the sheet
- You have heavy ink coverage across the folds
- Your folding style requires hand work
- You have concerns about critical fold placement or color breaks at the folds
- You want the highest-quality fold.

The general industry rule is to score 100# text weight and above, however, there can be situations where you may choose to score lighter weight sheets.

THERE ARE MANY WAYS TO SCORE

Letterpress score. Letterpress scoring is the highest quality and the most expensive. It is an offline process in which a steel rule is formed into the desired shape and set within a piece of wood that is locked onto a metal frame. The frame is clamped to a letterpress machine that forces the paper between the steel rule and the impression of the press. The process is slower, but the result is outstanding.

Rotary score. This process uses a special wheel attachment for folding machinery, and the wheel with pressure applied rolls as the sheet passes underneath prior to folding and creates the crease inline during the finishing process.

Litho score (press score). Press scores allow the application of a score inline while the job is on press. Metal rules with adhesive backing are applied to the impression cylinder on the press. The scoring rule creases the sheet as it passes underneath.

Wet score. This type of scoring is specifically for an uncoated sheet. A special water attachment on the folding machine applies a thin, straight stream of solution where the paper must fold. With dampness on the fold, the paper cannot help but create a perfectly clean fold.

Heat score. A litho scoring technique requiring the use of special offset presses that can hold heat. This process can apply up to 350°F (176.6°C) heat to a copper die that can score, stamp, or emboss inline during the printing process. Heat-scoring is especially effective on heavier-coated stocks, but is not good for dry, uncoated stocks as the heat removes moisture from the sheet.

Impact score (electronic knife). This is used primarily for short-run digital print. A knife with fixed-width steel rule and channel strikes the sheet to create a crease. This offers a die-quality crease, but is slower than other techniques due to the reciprocating action of the knife.

Rotary scoring cylinder applies pressure as sheet passes beneath. Image courtesy of www.TechnifoldUSA.com **(left)** *Letterpress dies embed steel rules into a piece of wood to stamp the shape onto the paper* **(above)**

FOLDING FOR DIGITAL PRINT

Digital print used to be a fairly restrictive process. It was great for short runs, smaller formats, and simple folding styles. Quality was good but not as good as offset, paper choice was limited, and the glossy look of the toner was unmistakable. Times have changed, however.

The line between digital and conventional print has blurred and digital is now better than ever. Not only has the quality become almost indistinguishable from offset print, the color is amazing, the variety of digitally-qualified papers has exploded, small format digital is moving to larger formats, and the technology of print finishing has caught up as well. High-speed automated folding machines execute highly complex direct mail pieces inline, taking them from a preprinted web to cut, fold, glue, and convert to a finished product in a single pass.

The technology of digital is its strength, as is the ability to create individualized print materials. There is tremendous value in using customer data to customize targeted mailings. This technique, called Variable Data Publishing (VDP) uses various software technologies to pull information from a database to customize the message or graphics in a printed piece. Combine VDP with other technologies such as Personalized URLs (PURLs) or QR codes, and behold—the power of print!

From a print finishing perspective, the biggest challenges with digital are static between the sheets, toner buildup on the rollers of the folding machine, and cracking on the fold. Your printer or print finisher will utilize industry-proven techniques to avoid these common issues.

One important note: not all printers have the same equipment, so don't make assumptions. Some printers have limitations of size and folding style, so ask a lot of questions.

QUESTIONS TO ASK YOUR PRINTER

- What is the maximum printable area of the sheet?
- Are there any technologies that might enhance my project, such as variable data or QR codes?
- Can my project benefit from any inline finishing processes that you offer?

- Are there any limitations from a folding perspective?
- Should I consider a varnish or coating to reduce the likelihood of scuffing?
- At what quantity would my project be better suited to offset printing?

FOLDING AND DIRECT MAIL

Folding and direct mail go hand-in-hand; however creating a folded direct mailpiece can be confusing, and the stakes are high. If you are not paying attention, you can make "small" mistakes that can destroy your profit margins. Here are a few production tips to help make your next direct mail project go off without a hitch:

- **Mind the aspect ratio.** The key to getting the best rates for direct mail is to stay within the aspect ratio requirements for letter-sized mail. There is a mathematical formula for this, but it is easier to get a free template from the post office and to simply place the piece on the template for a visual check.

- **Don't get cute with the address.** The address must always be parallel to the long dimension of the piece. Always. This enables the piece to be processed by machine.

- **Mock it up and weight it.** If you are even mildly concerned about the weight of the piece, don't take chances. Make a mock-up in the chosen stock—even throw the stamp on there (it affects the weight!) and put it on a postal scale to be sure you are safely within the weight (and thickness) guidelines.

Name
Address Line 1
Address Line 2
Address Liine 3

Wrong

Name
Address Line 1
Address Line 2
Address Liine 3

Right

Address placement should always be parallel to the long dimension of the piece (right)

- **Fold placement matters.** Look at the mailing panel of your mailpiece. The right edge is considered the lead edge. If the folds are vertical, there must be a fold rather than a tab at the lead edge. You will also be required to tab or glue the remaining open edges. If the fold is horizontal, the fold should be positioned below the address at the bottom edge.

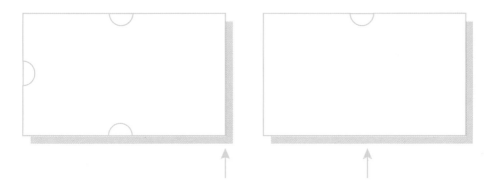

The postal service evaluates your mailpiece in three ways. Failure to qualify in the categories below can mean steep surcharges or even rejection:

1 **Mailability.** Can it be mailed? Does the piece meet the minimum size and thickness requirements to go through the mail?

2 **Machinability.** Can it be processed? Does the piece meet the proper aspect ratio (length divided by height), and is the address parallel to the longest dimension?

3 **Readability.** Can the machine identify it? Are the fonts readable? Is the artwork obstructing data? Is there enough contrast between paper/envelope color and text? Can the machine find the address?

DIRECT MAIL DESIGN TIPS
- **Do not confuse the recipient.** Have a clear message that grabs their attention and leads them through the piece.
- **Merge form and function.** A cool fold or paper, or other eye-catching technique, can be very effective, but the end result has to make sense.
- **Change your designs.** Keep the same look for too long and the recipient starts to think they have already seen what you have to offer. A different color or photo change does not count.

QUICK DIRECT MAIL TIPS

- Get a shape-based pricing template from the post office.
- Make a friend at the post office or a mail house.
- Stay within letter mail-size specifications at all costs.
- Make sure the address is parallel to the longest dimension.
- Fold placement should be along the bottom edge (below the address) or at the lead edge (to the right of the address).

DESIGNER'S TIP

Do not shoot yourself (or your client) in the foot before your mailpiece even hits the mailstream. Careless mistakes like improper sizing can send your mailing costs sky high for no good reason. Practice extreme consciousness when it comes to direct mail, choosing only optimal sizes and formats, and double-checking art preparation and fold placement to minimize postage expense.

This direct mailpiece from Neenah Paper is an oblong-format Roll Fold with an arrow-shaped die-cut on the cover. This piece would likely be tabbed top and bottom to go through the mail system.

CHOOSING THE RIGHT FOLD FOR YOUR PROJECT

One look through this book and you will feel newly inspired—possibly overwhelmed. The obvious question that comes up after a designer realizes just how many options they have is: "How do I know which folding style is the best choice for my project?" The answer relies on a mix of instinct, elimination, and organization.

There are several questions to answer at the beginning of the process that will help you to rule in/rule out certain folding styles.

Is the content you are working with text-heavy, and must that content be read in a particular order? Or is the content image-heavy with shorter "nuggets" of information?
If a large body of text must be read in a particular order, rule out the Roll Fold. The rolling panels can cause confusion as to the order in which the material should be read. If it is text-light and image-heavy, you can do a lot. Gate Folds and Roll Folds offer a great reveal; Accordions are fun; and if you have the budget, a Specialty Fold makes sense if the concept lends itself to a special solution.

Is the piece going to be mailed or inserted into an envelope?
Accordion Folds are notorious for trouble during auto-insertion into envelopes and, because they do not have a closed edge, they generally require four wafer seals when produced as a self-mailer. If you love the Accordion, and you are sending it through the mail or inserting it, try a Wrapped Accordion (see page 80) instead. Specialty Folds, due to their uniqueness in shape or form, can also require hand-insertion and special mailing considerations. Talk to a printer, your mail house, or postal design professional for guidance.

Who is your audience?
Think about the recipient's experience with the piece. If your audience is elderly, do not choose something that could be confusing to fold back down to size. Mind your paper finishes, too—choice of a super glossy sheet can cause glare and make it difficult to read. If your audience is creative, their standards for design are high and you

could have success with something unique, or catch their eye with a special paper. If your audience is conservative or academic, they tend to seek order and may be frustrated by a loose design grid.

What is the purpose and the mood of the piece?
Are you telling a story, promoting a product, inviting someone to an event, or calling for action? Is the mood serious, celebratory, humorous, or confident? Each of these scenarios affect the pacing, style, and distribution of content, and can influence the choice of folding style.

What is your budget?
You knew we had to go there. Of course, budget has to play a role in choice of folding style. The good news is that there are great things that can be done on low and high budgets. If you are stuck in the low budget category, try a simple guillotine trim to shorten the cover, rotate it, or change the format from upright to oblong. Small adjustments can make all the difference.

After you answer these questions, you should be able to eliminate some of the choices and start to hone in on your selection. From here, organization is key. Start to think about how you want your audience to experience the piece.
- Do you want the content slowly revealed (possibly Accordion, Tri-Fold, Parallel)?
- Do you want the viewer to experience surprise somewhere (possibly Gate, Poster, Specialty)?

Lastly, instinct comes into play.
- Looking at the content you have to work with, what folding style *feels* right?
- Which folding style seems to fit with the design concept and content?

And finally, one more word of wisdom: success relies on the proper choice of fold, distribution and styling of content, paper choice, and placement of critical marketing messages. The best folded print materials utilize folding as a *component* of the overall design concept and delivery, and not as a gimmick.

ORDER OF OPENING: PLACING YOUR CRITICAL MARKETING MESSAGE

When designing for folded materials, there is more to consider than just folding style, paper choice, layout, color palette, and typeface. What most people don't realize is that each folding style has a different user experience that is not driven by the layout, but rather by the instinctive opening order of that given folding style.

A great example would be to compare a Closed Gate Fold with a Roll Fold. Starting with the Closed Gate Fold, if you put a critical marketing message on the inside right panel (see illustration 1), the message will likely be viewed if thoughtfully designed, and the recipient will continue to open up the two gate panels to reveal the interior spread. Alternately, if you were to change your folding style to a Roll Fold (see illustration 2), keeping the layout scheme the same with the critical marketing message on the interior right panel, the message may very well be completely overlooked. Why, you ask? The reason is that general behavior with a Roll Fold is to roll it out immediately to look at the interior spread. If this is true, your critical marketing message has just landed on the back of the brochure. And if you put something important on the face of the most interior roll panel, you're really asking for trouble.

There are factors that can possibly change the natural pattern of behavior, such as a very bright color or image, huge text, or other blatant distraction technique, but that's not always a safe bet, so here's a great tip. Whenever you design something folded, mock it up, hand it to several people individually, and watch them experience the piece. Don't tell them why you're handing it to them, and don't ask them to find the marketing message. When they hand it back to you, ask them what they took away from the piece. Did they get your marketing message? In what order did they view the content? Did they know what the piece was about and what to do with it? What is intuitive to you may not be intuitive to your audience, and the results may surprise you. If they didn't get the message, you should rethink your layout and content.

1. Closed Gate Fold with critical message on right interior panel

2. Roll Fold with critical message on right interior panel

GALLERY

Snake Folds produced by ColorCraft of Virginia

*The Pop-out Accordion
uses short scores and die-cuts
for dimension*

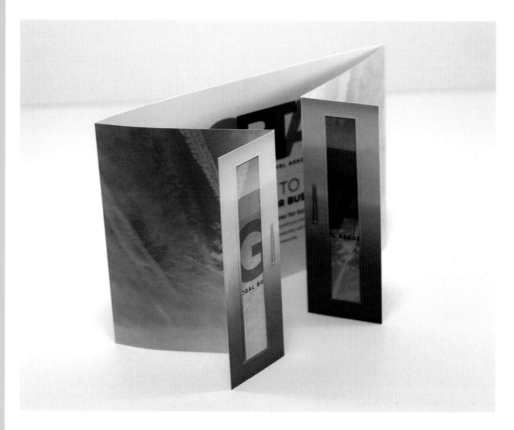

*Open Gate Fold with short
panels produced by ITP*

Don't miss
this opportunity to
be a part of one of the most
exciting and informative business
functions of the year. Please mark your
calendar now and reserve September 22-25 for
this important event. Watch for your
registration information
package in the mail!

Save the Date!

Tulip Fold by ColorCraft of Virginia **(left)** *Petal Fold by Kanella Arapoglou* **(below)**

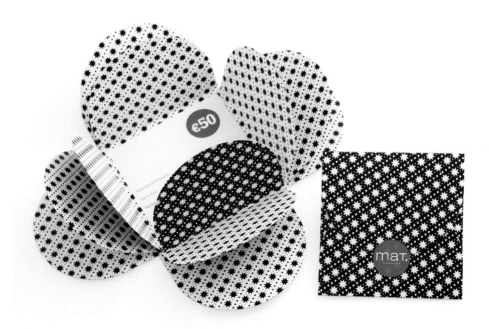

CHAPTER TWO: BREAK OUT OF YOUR FOLDING RUT

If you ask a room full of designers or printers to name some folding styles, you will always get the same answers—Tri-Fold, Roll Fold, Gate Fold, Accordion Fold, and sometimes on a rare occasion someone will say Map Fold or Parallel Fold. Wouldn't it be nice to hear someone shout "Iron Cross!" or "Triple Parallel!" with some enthusiasm?

This sad experiment is living proof of a worldwide epidemic—the folding rut. The good news is that it is an easy condition to remedy. There are some very simple things you can do to freshen up the old stand-bys you work with every day, and many of these solutions do not involve a substantial jump in the budget—just some consideration and a little creativity.

On the following pages, you will find an assortment of tips and techniques to help you make your next folded brochure stand out in a sea of sameness.

TAP YOUR RESOURCES

Printers and print finishers are a great resource for ideas. Just because they are not technically considered creatives, they can be very creative when it comes to producing challenging work. If you are feeling stale, ask your printer or bindery for some samples of interesting folded brochures they have made, or see if they will let you loose in their sample room.

Great places to find creative folding samples:

• *Watch your mail. Some pretty neat things get thrown away every day, so look before you shred. Pay attention to how things fold, their size and shape, and whether or not the piece survived the mailing process. Save the things you like.*

• *Promotional materials from paper companies are high in production value and very creative. Foldability is a critical issue for paper, so the companies are often finding creative ways to showcase this feature.*

• *For instant online inspiration, visit foldfactory.com's 3-D sample library. View hundreds of short videos of folded solutions. Watch them fold and unfold.*

• *Check out art galleries, theater events, and museum exhibits. Visual and performing arts often promote themselves with great design.*

• *Tourist information areas always have a wall of brochures. Just make sure you give yourself some time to peruse.*

COVER TRICKS AND TRIMS

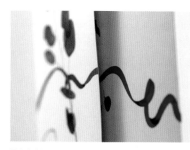

If you want to make your brochure stand out from the rest, sometimes you do not have to look much further than the cover. The cover of a folded brochure—much like the cover of a book—often determines whether it will be opened or examined at all. There are many ways to add interest to the cover that go beyond typography, color, and imagery. Great design plus a few little tricks can make all the difference.

Tri-fold with short cover by Molly McCoy

1 **Simple guillotine trims.** A short trim on the cover panel lets the contents of the panel below show through, and from a production standpoint, it does not add to the cost because it is not a die-cut. Use a shot of bright color; run large text up the side on the panel below and let the cover visually chop the edge of the text; give a sneak preview of an exciting image hidden behind the cover.

2 **Angled guillotine trims.** For the right design concept, an angled trim on the cover panel can look edgy or avant-garde. Again, this is just a guillotine trim, but it is a bit more involved than a simple (straight) trim because the printer has to create a jig to angle the paper in the cutter, and the angled trim could make the fold more difficult to manufacture by machine, depending upon the folding style. Always talk with your printer before choosing solutions with angled trims or angled folds.

1

2

3 **Die-cut cover shape.** Take it up a notch
by adding a die-cut to the cover. It can be
visually interesting to turn the cover panel
into a shape, for example a half-circle. This
creates a nice contrast with the rectangular
or square format of panels beneath it, and
the addition of a hard shape can inspire
different creative solutions or graphic
elements in the layout that may not
have been entertained when the shape
was rectangular.

4 **Die-cut shapes on the cover.** Maybe a
large shaped cover is not what you are
looking for, but adding a die-cut window or
geometric shape (or cluster of shapes) can
be a very effective cover enhancement. It is
a lot of fun to let color or image tease and
entice the recipients to open the brochure.
Just be sure the "payoff" is there, or they
will lose interest.

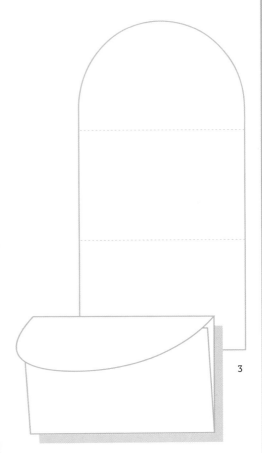

3

4

Iron Cross Fold with layered
die by Whitmore Group

5   **Locked cover solutions.** These are fun.
    There are different ways that the cover of
    a folded piece can interact with another
    panel to "lock" the piece closed. The most
    common way to do this is by adding a
    centered vertical slit half the finished
    height of the piece ascending up from
    the bottom edge of the cover, and a similar
    slit descending from the top of a facing
    panel. When the two are combined, they
    lock together. The result can also be
    dimensional. This type of cover solution
    always requires hand work, which adds
    to the production cost.

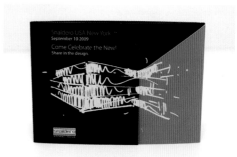

Locked Letter Fold with angled die by
Gina Vivona, GV Creative

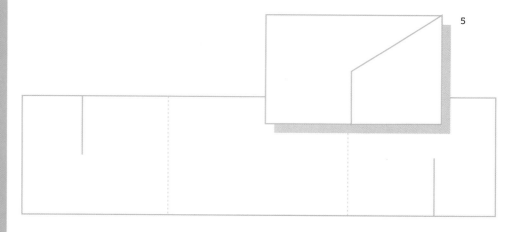

5

Locked Gate fold holiday card
by Davidson Belluso

BROADSIDE FOLDS

A Broadside Fold doubles its area because the sheet is folded in half before any characteristic folding takes place. This style of folding adds several benefits to a folded brochure—extra real estate for graphics and information, a more substantial or quality feel because of the added thickness of doubling a sheet, and of course creative opportunities.

The most common use for the large interior spread is as a poster or map.

Broadside Folds are fairly straightforward in their format, but for their simplicity, the level of production difficulty increases with the addition of right-angle folds. For example, a standard Tri-Fold consists of two parallel folds, which is very simple. Turn the same folding style into a Broadside Fold, and you are looking at one parallel fold and two right-angle folds.

Right-angle folds require additional or different machinery configuration, or a second pass through the machine due to a change in direction of the folds. There is also greater concern over paper choice when right-angles are concerned, as a heavier sheet will create wrinkles in the corner joints of the folds, so ask your printer or paper representative for a suggested weight or for paper dummies in the weights you are considering.

FAST FACT
Broadside folding has often been called French folding. Truth is, a French Fold is actually a design decision. French Folds are Broadside Folds that are printed only on one side—the outside—leaving the other side, the side that is ultimately the interior poster spread, blank. French Folds are common for fancy invitations and special occasions.

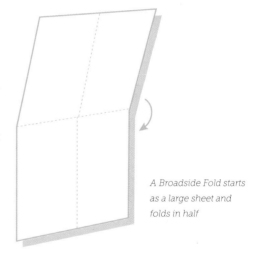

A Broadside Fold starts as a large sheet and folds in half

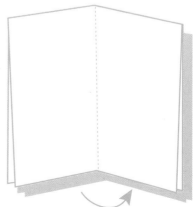

Once folded in half, the Broadside format can take many shapes

LONG PANELS

Asymmetrical Accordion with long trailing panel by Barbara Cooper Design **(above and right)**

Often in the pursuit of the "different", we can look as if we are trying too hard. The good news is, not all the tricks of the trade are blatantly bold—as a matter of fact, some folding techniques tend to whisper rather than scream for attention. Whispers are good when you are looking to project an image of understated elegance, or to simply complement the content rather than upstage it with a gimmick.

The extension of a trailing panel creates a step that extends past the cover. The effect is quite different from, say, a simple guillotine trim on the cover. Both create a visual contrast that extends past the cover panel. The short trim relates directly to the content on the panel below it, whereas the extended trailing panel is not an extension of the cover. While it is close to the cover visually when the piece is folded, it is physically an extension of a back cover panel.

The fun of this technique is that it can be frivolous or utilitarian in application. There are occasions where it might be appropriate to treat the extension as a tab and put descriptive text on it, or maybe use it to isolate a logo. The space can also just be solid color or textured as a creative element.

Trailing panel (far right) is wider than the other panels

Want to get fancy? Then add a die-cut to the edge of the extended panel.

There are always exceptions, but in most cases, from a production standpoint, this technique does not add to cost because the trailing panel is the final panel to go through the folding machine and, being slightly longer, does not affect the machine setup.

This technique works well for Accordion Folds and Double Parallel Folds in particular, due to the fact that they have open trailing edges, as opposed to Roll Folds, Tri-Folds and Gate Folds, whose panels tuck into themselves.

Accordion with
long trailing panel

Double parallel with long
trailing panel

SHORT FOLDS

Short Folds are an exciting solution for modifying the Broadside format of folding. The difference between the two is that instead of folding the sheet in half so that all panels are the same height, a Short Fold is folded short of halfway so that half the panels are shorter than the others. How much shorter is up to you.

And here is where it becomes fun. Short Folds offer all kinds of creative opportunities because of their flexibility. First of all, you can Short Fold to the inside or outside of the piece. What this means is that you can either have the Short Fold show up on the cover and outside of the piece, or you can reveal the Short Fold when the piece is opened.

Furthermore, creating a short trim on a brochure isolates a thin strip of space that can be used as a focal point for a teaser or headline, or a series of photos or graphics.

You can even flip a Short Fold and create an Inverted Short Fold. Inverted Short Folds pull downward rather than lifting up. These, too, can be to the interior or exterior of the piece. The inverted format, more so than the standard format, offers an additional benefit: utility. An Inverted Short Fold can become a glueless pocket to nest additional light materials, such as a sell sheet or a folded brochure.

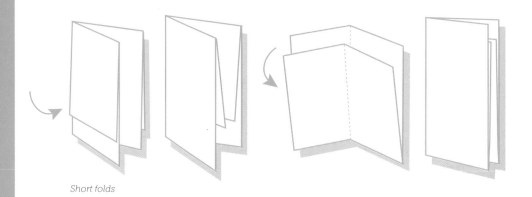

Short folds

DIE-CUTS AND TRIMS

A whole book could be written about die-cuts alone, as the creative opportunities are truly endless. The wonderful thing about die-cutting is its versatility—it can be used sparingly for an understated effect, or it can be what drives the layout and the entire experience of the piece.

The die-cut can provide a special detail, like rounded corners on an Accordion Fold, or a decorative element, like small clusters of circles or an identifiable organic shape. The die-cut can be created for utility, as a closing mechanism, or as a business card holder.

Some of the wildest Specialty Folds involve die-cutting to create special panel shapes and sizes, and a unique viewer experience. Many Specialty Folds that involve complex die-cutting also require scoring and potentially hand-folding.

Accordion Fold with blue whale die for Smithsonian National Museum of Natural History. Designed by Kate Meyers and Jesse Wellenbring. Images courtesy of Smithsonian NMNH

Accordion Fold with custom die-cut center panel

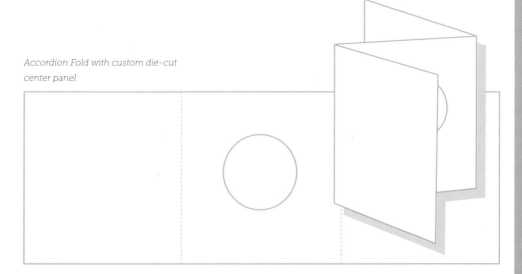

TIP

Practice self control! Think about what you want and about your design concept before you look through the printer's pre-enjoyed dies. It is similar to shopping the clearance rack at a clothes store, where you find something that is not really your style, but as the price is good you force it to work, and then end up looking ridiculous. The same rule applies to die shopping. Do not grab the circle-shaped Gate Fold die because the Iron Cross die was not the right size. Ask a few printers or proactively search so you know who has what, and then keep those ideas in your back pocket for future projects.

SPLURGE OR SAVE

Die-cuts are often considered a splurge, since they are an additional, and usually offline, finishing process. If you are on a limited budget but have a little padding in there, ask your printer if they have any interesting dies you could look through. You may be able to use someone else's Iron Cross die, or other Specialty Fold, and eliminate the cost of creating the die while getting the unusual folded solution you are looking for. Remember that the cost of the die is one part of it, but the offline process of die-cutting would still be your responsibility.

"DIE-CUT" ON THE CHEAP

A guillotine trim is not a die-cut, but done the right way it can sure look like one. An easy way to add some pizzazz without the cost is to use an angled guillotine trim.

This example uses the clever placement of two angled cuts placed on opposing corners. When folded down or opened flat, the shape is distinctive. Take that same corner cut concept and use it on one corner of one interior panel of a Broadside Fold, and you have a triangle-shaped visual teaser inviting you to lift to reveal the large poster spread.

Add an angled guillotine trim to the top of an Accordion Fold for an Angled Accordion Fold (see pages 78–79), or throw an angle on an extended trailing panel of an Accordion or Double Parallel Fold, or to a short trim on a cover to shake things up.

Angled Accordion by Upshift Creative Group

QUANTITY AND AUTOMATION

Almost any folding style can be produced by machine if there is a high enough quantity. In many cases, a Specialty Fold is finished by hand because it is not worth the time and effort involved in re-engineering the machines necessary to automate the process. If you are producing folded materials in very large quantities—hundreds of thousands or into the millions—you may be surprised at the interesting solutions you can use for your printed materials. There are some very skilled specialty binderies that can do amazing things by machine—Twist Folds, Iron Crosses, Swingers, and much more—and if your fold cannot be automated, there are printers with very large hand-bindery departments that can accomplish large volumes within a very quick time frame.

EXTRA TIP

It pays to ask. If you are scoring, ask your printer what scoring method they are using because there are many ways to score. Here is why we ask: if they are using a letterpress score, they are making a custom die. So, it is possible to add cutting and perforating to that die, often at only a small additional charge.

Accordion with angled guillotine-cut corners by Design Ranch

GLUELESS POCKETS

Folding techniques, or the combination of folding and die-cutting, can be a useful method when you are looking to avoid an additional finishing process, such as gluing. Each process can add up, so if you can cleverly eliminate one, you can save some money.

INVERTED SHORT FOLD

The simplest way to create a glueless pocket is with an Inverted Short Fold. The pocket depth is up to you, but the result is the ability to nest materials on the interior or exterior of the piece. This technique does not work with every folding style, so experiment. The best formula for success with an Inverted Short Fold pocket is to be sure you have at least one fold-in panel so that the right and left edges that form the center pocket area are closed and have some tension. If you try to do this with a four-pager, or with a Double Parallel or Accordion, your materials will fall out because the format of the fold is too open. The best choices for this technique are Tri-Folds, Roll Folds, Gate Folds, and some Parallel Fold formats.

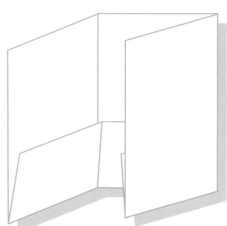

Letter Fold with inverted short fold glueless pocket on interior

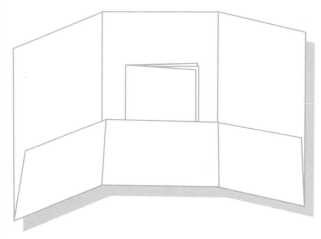

Inverted short fold creates a "pocket" to hold light materials

ANGLED FOLD

With some experimentation, an Angled Fold
can also create a glueless pocket. Create an
Inverted Broadside Fold (fold at the bottom) so
that the open edge is at the top. Then take one
of the exterior panels and fold it inward on the
diagonal to create a pocket. The right edge will
remain open unless you get creative with the
format of the Broadside Fold and make the
diagonal fold long and wide so that you can
fold and close the edge. This technique is great
for binding a glueless pocket into a spiral or
twin-wire mechanical binding.

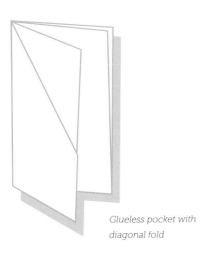

*Glueless pocket with
diagonal fold*

CREATIVE DIE-CUTTING

There are always great opportunities with
custom die-cuts, as you can make any shape
you want and get creative with format. The
possibilities are endless, but the example
shown above right creates two flaps—one that
folds up and one that folds over. Each flap has
a slit in it, and one ultimately fits into the other
to form the pocket. The result is a sturdy
glueless pocket.

PRODUCTION NOTE

Here's an interesting glueless pocket
solution that utilizes a score and die cut.
The locking mechanism eliminates glue,
but requires hand-folding to finish.
In a small quantity, if you want to fold the
pockets by yourself, you will save money.

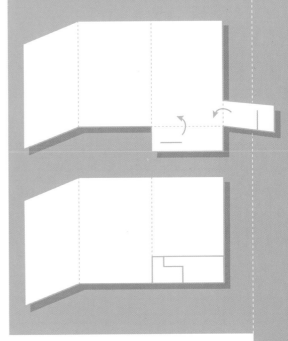

SHORT FLAPS

A short flap is a panel that measures less than half the dimension in width or height in comparison to the other panels of the folded piece. Flaps serve as closing mechanisms for direct mail when folded to the exterior, and as tear-off coupons, business reply cards, or other functional elements when folded to the interior.

There are very few rules regarding short flaps and their use, which opens the door to many creative solutions, including interesting die-cuts or tear-off ideas, and even testimonials. When used for direct mail, short flaps must be either glued or tabbed to seal the edges for machinability.

You can add short flaps to many different folding styles, including four-pagers, Tri-Folds, Rolls, Accordions, Gates, and more. From a production standpoint, flaps generally do not increase the level of difficulty of the folding style, so adding a flap can be an easy way to change up your next project.

Short flap folding to the interior

Short flap folding to the exterior

DESIGNER TIP

If you choose to shorten the fold-in panels of a Closed Gate fold, the level of difficulty will increase dramatically if the gap between the two panels is greater than 2in (50.8mm).

Vertical format tri-fold with short flap cover panel by Gina Vivona, GV Creative.

DESIGNER TIP

Flaps can be a really fun way to get the viewer to interact with imagery. A short flap can cover part of an image, or duplicate part of an image in exact registration with an image printed on the panel that lies beneath it. When the flap is lifted, something is added or subtracted from the image for a visual trick. Another option is to interact the recipient with the image. For example, there could be an image of a phone on its cradle on the short flap. When the flap is opened, the reverse of the flap is the underside of the phone (as if the recipient had picked it up), with the image on the panel below the flap revealing an empty cradle.

ROTATION AND FORMAT CHANGES

Sometimes just a change in format or direction is enough to make your project feel fresh and new. The next time you are feeling creatively stale and looking for a quick and economical solution, try the following rotation technique.

Instead of making a standard 4 x 9in (101.6 x 228.6mm) Tri-Fold brochure, try flipping the width and height measurements by making a 9 x 4in (228.6 x 101.6mm) Tri-Fold instead. See the difference? Same size and folding style, but a very different layout and viewer experience.

Before you change format on a project, do some research. Some projects are in a certain format for a reason—for example, they may be designed to fit into literature holders, or into a standard envelope, or file folder. They also might be part of an existing series of pieces that must look uniform as a set.

Standard 4 x 9 Tri-Fold

TIP

Bear in mind that if you are creating a self-mailing piece, you will need to look very carefully at what the rotation change did to fold placement, as the latter has a lot to do with the ability to process the mailpiece by machine. For more information about fold placement as it relates to direct mail, see pages 34–36.

Change of format is another option. If most of your projects are a classic upright format, maybe you can switch to oblong, square, or narrow to change things up.

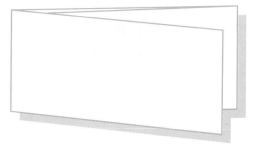

9 x 4 oblong format Tri-Fold

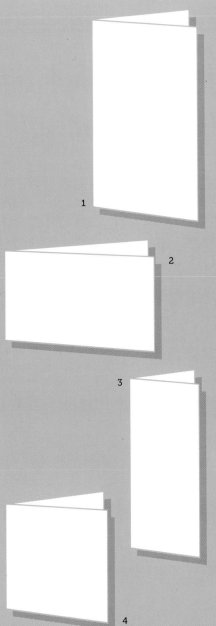

FORMAT OPTIONS

There are four basic folding formats: upright, oblong, narrow, and square. Certain measurement ratios, described below, will qualify a given folded piece as a specific format.

1 **Upright.** To qualify as an upright format, the finished height of the folded piece must be more than ¾in (19mm) greater than the finished width. Some common upright dimensions are 5 x 8in (127 x 203.2mm) or 4 x 6in (101.6 x 152.4mm).

2 **Oblong.** To qualify as an oblong format, the finished width of the piece must be more than ¾in (19mm) greater than the finished height. Some common oblong dimensions are 6 x 4in (152.4 x 101.6mm) or 8 x 5in (203.2 x 127mm). There are special considerations for an oblong format piece—check with the printer or print finisher about the minimum height capabilities of the folding machinery.

3 **Narrow.** To qualify as a narrow format, the finished height must be at least twice the finished width. Some common narrow dimensions are 4 x 8in (101.6 x 203.2mm) or 3 x 9in (76.2 x 228.6mm). There are special considerations for a narrow format piece— check with the printer or print finisher about the minimum width capabilities of the folding machinery.

4 **Square.** To qualify as a square format, the difference between the finished height and finished width cannot be more than (+/-) ¾in (19mm). Some common square dimensions are 6 x 6in (152.4 x 152.4mm) or 6 x 5½ in (152.4 x 139.7mm).

ASYMMETRY

Often when we fold, we aim to create the appearance of symmetry, but asymmetry is a great technique for changing things up from a folding perspective.

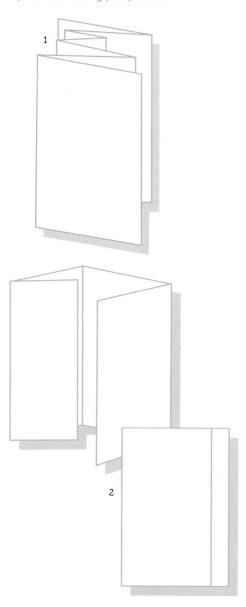

What is most distracting (in a good way) about an asymmetrical folding solution is that we see so much of the same every day, that often all it takes is a subtle change in symmetry to get the viewer's attention. Here are a few great examples to try:

1   An Accordion Fold with panels of different lengths becomes—you guessed it—an Asymmetrical Accordion Fold. These can be a lot of fun to work with, and the shorter Accordion panels are great for interesting imagery or testimonials/quotes. The key to the success of this style is to shorten the panels in pairs or it will not finish flush.

2   You can make an Asymmetrical Closed Gate Fold by making the two leftmost panels shorter than the two rightmost panels (with the fold-in panels slightly shorter to . accommodate for the dimensionality of the sheet). The result is a stepped cover effect.

3   Take a Gate Fold and push the gap between the fold-in panels to off-center. Fresh!

4   You can make an Asymmetrical Roll Fold by making the cover and back cover panels the same width, and making the roll-in panels much narrower than normal. The effect feels like a four-pager with a mini Roll Fold on the interior.

As always, consult a printer early on as you are exploring unconventional formats and techniques. Some asymmetrical adjustments can be automated, others cannot.

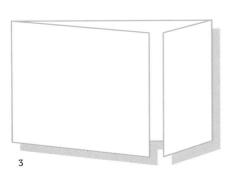

Asymmetrical Accordion by Maureen Weiss Design **(above)**
Stepped Double-Parallel design and illustration by Kelsey Grafton **(left)**

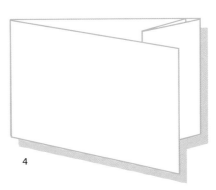

3

4

SPECIALTY AND PROPRIETARY FOLDED SOLUTIONS

WHAT MAKES A FOLD "SPECIALTY"?

Specialty folding refers to anything that is unconventional. Conventional folding is considered anything that can be finished on standard fare bindery equipment by a moderately skilled bindery professional. Unconventional can refer to size, substrate, folding configuration, extremely high quantities requiring unusual production capacity and inline processes, the need for specialized equipment and highly skilled technicians to execute the fold, or the inability to produce the fold by machine.

PRODUCTION NOTE

Gate Folds are *not* Specialty Folds, so do not believe the myth. There was a time when finding a vendor with the right equipment to produce a Gate Fold by machine was challenging—to get around this, the final fold had to be done by hand, which added a lot of cost. Times have changed and modern printers have more in-house equipment than they used to, and there is more than one way to mechanically fold a Gate (not to mention some pretty cool computerized folding machines that make quick work of them). These days, Gate Folds are actually quite common and affordable.

PopOut®

Z-CARD® PocketMedia

WHERE IS THE LINE?

Some details that seem like small issues can turn a standard project into a difficult or specialty project. Here are a few basic rules to help define the line between standard and specialty folding:

- Miniature folding: one dimension smaller than 2in (50.8mm).
- Oversized folding: a fold longer than 30in (762mm).
- Accordions with more than six parallel folds, Rolls with more than five panels, Closed Gates with a gap wider than 2in (50.8mm), Gates with an overlap of less than ¼in (6.35mm), or no gap at all.
- Folds on the diagonal, odd shapes like circles and triangles, die-cut multi-directional folding, stepped folds without a flush edge.
- Extremely lightweight/delicate papers, or extremely heavy papers.

PROPRIETARY FOLDED SOLUTIONS

There are companies in the market that have developed unique folded solutions and patented or named them. The patented solutions are called "proprietary solutions" and the named solutions are considered "branded solutions." If the solution is patented, in many cases you must work with the patent holder to be able to use that fold for your project. Most exotic (specialty) folds are not patented. To determine if the folding style you are considering is patented, simply look for a patent number on the folded piece to be sure.

Branded solutions are innovative, marketed solutions and if they are not patented, you can recreate the solution, but you cannot adopt the brand name. There are, however, many benefits to working through a patent holder or marketer of a branded solution—often they have refined the efficiencies of producing the products and can be very competitive from a production and pricing standpoint. Many also offer templates and design services, a skilled team of marketing consultants, and sophisticated technologies to further enhance the product and ROI.

There are lots of exciting proprietary and branded solutions on the market today. Do not let the proprietary nature of these folding styles scare you away. Some of these solutions can cost a bit more (or potentially even less) than a conventional project, depending upon quantity and other factors; however, considering the increased response rate you can expect if sent to a targeted list, the true value is hard to ignore.

Here is just a sample of some interesting patented/branded solutions:

1. The Book-Cube™
Status: exclusive (patented) branded solution
Offered by: Structural Graphics/Essex, CT
Website: structuralgraphics.com
The Book-Cube™ is a great example of utilizing the element of surprise to get the recipient's attention. This design ships flat, usually as a direct mail piece, and when the envelope, or other carrier such as an iron cross, is opened, it immediately pops into a 3-dimensional cube shape. The cube can be transformed into a save-the-date, an ornament, a CD/DVD/USB media carrier, a tchotchke—there are lots of creative opportunities. The Book-Cube™ is completely customizable in size and shape, and is also available through Structural Graphics quick-turn line of products sold under the RocketShip® brand.

2. Jaguar
Status: proprietary solution
Offered by: B.Moss
Website: b-moss.com
Some creative folded marketing solutions focus on the reveal to create powerful marketing materials. And when you can get the recipient involved in that process, it's much more effective. The Jaguar has a sliding pull-out panel that reveals an image through a window. The magic, however, is in the slider panel. One would think that, when pulled to the right, the slider panel would just have the original image from the window on it, but the slider also reveals a surprise.

3. The Flapper®
Status: proprietary (patented) solution
Offered by: Structural Graphics/Essex, CT
Website: structuralgraphics.com
The Flapper® is a solution that has been a favorite among advertisers for years—four selling panels that turn in succession to tell a marketing story in an interactive, engaging, and addictive way. The affordable, extremely versatile design can be used as a self-mailer, a magazine insert, or a premium; and can include inkjet imaging, scents, scratch-offs, bar codes, and bonus compartments. One warning: once you start the Flapper®, you may not be able to stop.

4. InteliMailer (also called Transformailer)
Status: exclusive branded solution
Offered by: Acculink
Website: www.intelimailer.com
A direct mail solution that uses a unique single-sheet format to create both a full-color envelope and insert in one pass. One of the cooler things about this solution is the shape of the envelope—it is folded on the diagonal, so the appearance is unique and hard to resist. Transformailers are economical to produce and can be personalized with variable text and images, sticky notes, PURLs, QR codes, or Microsoft Tag glyphs to connect the printed direct mail to smartphone, online, mobile, and social marketing content.

5. PopOut®
Status: Exclusive branded solution modeled after patented retail product
Offered by: PopOut Products
Website: popoutproducts.com
The PopOut® is a high-impact dimensional marketing solution. The beauty of this product is its amazing ability to finish flat and to expand into a burst of graphics when opened. PopOuts® are fully customizable and offered in several formats, sizes, and options including single and double PopOuts®, PopOuts® with stitched booklets, and even a self-mailer. Although often typecast as a map solution due to its close association to PopOut City Maps, the PopOut® doesn't have to be a map. It is

1. *The Book-Cube™*

3. *The Flapper®*

4. *InteliMailer*

5. *PopOut®*

wonderful for large graphics or any promotional information. There is a tremendous amount of creative potential with this product and it is a perfect marketing tool for any brand.

6. ShowStopper™
Status: proprietary solution
Patent #'s 7,490,425 and D556,830
Offered by: 3D Paper Graphics
Website: 3dpapergraphics.com
Dimensional mail has been shown to generate higher response rates than traditional flat advertising, so why not make the most of it? Collapsed, the ShowStopper™ from 3D Paper Graphics fits neatly into a mailable carrier. The recipient opens the piece, pulls out the ShowStopper™, and a self-standing keepsake is revealed. Increase brand awareness, create a memorable event invitation, a collectible series, or simply surprise and entertain with a powerful message that pops.

7. UVIAUS Pop-up
Status: proprietary solution
Offered by: UVIAUS
Website: uviaus.com
The UVIAUS Pop-up is a custom 3-dimensional pop-up card that promises to stand out among a sea of 2-dimensional print campaigns. The formats are based upon either a parallel fold (90 degree) or a V-fold (180 degree) pop-up configuration. UVIAUS offers a range of sizes and attention getting form factors that can fit virtually any budget, and they offer assistance in choosing the appropriate options to fit the needs of your project. The UVIAUS product line features offline and online creative solutions that make lasting impressions.

8. Video-In-Print®
Status: proprietary solution
Offered by: Americhip
Website: americhip.com
Studies prove that interacting with a brand on a sensory level will increase brand recall and mindshare exponentially, so why risk the chance that your marketing package will be flat and forgettable? The Video-In-Print® solution by Americhip embeds a multisensory print and media experience directly into your print materials—via video monitors that range from 1.8in all the way up to 10in—ensuring a positive and memorable experience.

9. Z-CARD® PocketMedia®
Status: exclusive branded solution, patented production process
Offered by: Z-CARD North America
Website: zcardna.com
Many have seen Z-CARDs® before, but there's a misconception that they're just for maps. The Z-CARD PocketMedia® format is one that lends itself to any situation where you need to fit a large amount of information into a small package. Z-CARDs® are also great for direct mail. For example, create a simple folded card and affix a Z-CARD® to the interior. The recipient can easily remove the Z-CARD® from the mailpiece and keep it. End cards can be rectangular or cut into custom shapes. Z-CARD® North America has mastered the automated production of their product and can offer small quantities up to quantities in the millions very efficiently. They can also accept printed materials and convert them into format.

8. *Video-In-Print®*

6. *Showstopper™*

7. *UVIAUS Pop-up*

9. *Z-CARD® PocketMedia*

GALLERY

Roll Fold with inverted short fold glueless pocket and accordion insert produced by Whitmore Group

*Tri-Fold with short trim
on cover and die-cut tab
by Premier Press and
Sandstrom Partners*

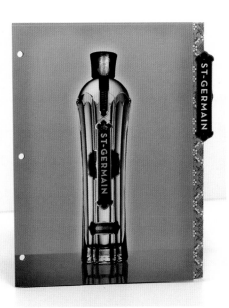

*Meandering Accordion by
Design Ranch*

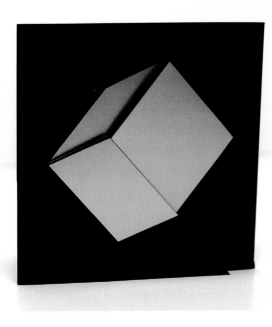

*Tri-Fold with die cut and foil
stamp by Publicis New York*

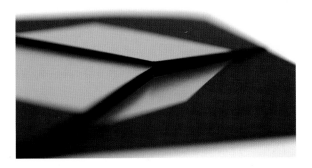

CHAPTER THREE: FUN FOLDS ON A BUDGET

Everybody has a budget. High or low, it's there. For most designers, the high budget project tends to be the happy break that comes along a few times a year. The rest of the year is filled with practical, yet still rewarding, projects that have to come in at (or ideally under) a conservative budget. And even with really tight budgets, it is generally expected that the end product will still be of the highest quality and creatively presented. So, how can you break out of the box without breaking the bank?

Budgets can be confining, and oftentimes designers feel stifled, as though they can't do anything creative under such restriction. That's why there are so many Tri-Folds in circulation. In fact, there are businesses whose entire profit center is built on Tri-Folds—quick printing, templates, pre-designed layouts. The Tri-Fold is the tried and true budget champion, a safe choice for any project. But is it really the only economical choice? No.

There are many different folds that can be produced in an economical manner—you just need to understand your options. The folding samples in this chapter are all in the low-to-moderate production price range. You'll soon find that there is an abundance of ways to shake up the everyday.

Get to know your printer

Most designers have a handful of favorite printers that they award their work to. But how well do you know your printers? How much do you know about their capabilities?

Conduct an interview with your favorite print providers (and maybe a few new ones). You may find that they have broader capabilities and services than you were aware of. Alternately, you may find that others are better suited to certain types of projects.

Questions to ask:

• *What is your greatest strength as a company?*

• *What sets you apart from other printers?*

• *Do you like a challenge?*

• *Have you added any new machinery or services?*

• *Do you offer any technologies that might improve my products or response, such as QR codes, variable data, mailing services, list management, etc.?*

• *Can I call you if I need help with a creative concept?*

• *May I have a tour?*

ANGLED ACCORDION FOLD

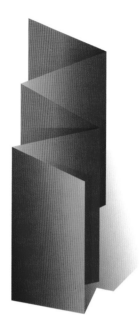

Suggested uses:
Special events
Promotion
Marketing collateral
Brochures

The Angled Accordion is a great example of using simple guillotine trims to create the look of a specialized die-cut. The angled trim works with the back-and-forth nature of the Accordion style of folding, and builds a graphic visual texture.

The severity of the angle chosen by the designer can greatly affect the appearance of the visual pattern. A very shallow angle will create little more than a decorative edge along the top, whereas a steep angle will create large triangular shapes and even the possibility of tabs or other graphics on each panel. Experiment with the angle to achieve the look you desire.

PRODUCTION TIP
It is most helpful to the printer if you make a separate layer in your digital document and call it "Angled Trim—Do Not Print." Draw an angled line exactly where you want the piece to be trimmed. It does not matter if the trim layer is on page 1 or page 2 of the document; however, if there is critical alignment on either side, choose the side with critical alignment. Also, if there are heavy areas of ink coverage, be sure to extend the color past the edge of the trim line just as you would for the bleed.

BUDGET SPLURGE
If you have some extra padding in the budget and a concept that calls for something really special, add a complex die-cut to the Angled Accordion. Rather than an angled guillotine trim, create an angled complex die that illustrates a scene or shapes. The zig-zag nature of the panels, when combined, will create a fabulous layered texture, and an interesting and artful reveal when opened.

DIGITAL DOCUMENT SIDE 1

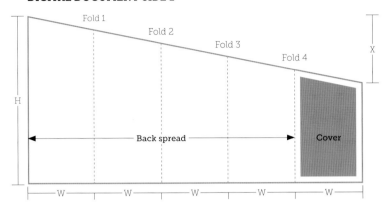

Fold 1 · Fold 2 · Fold 3 · Fold 4

H · X

Back spread · Cover

W — W — W — W — W

DIGITAL DOCUMENT SIDE 2

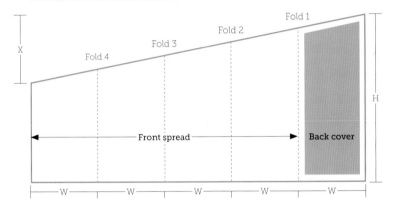

Fold 1 · Fold 2 · Fold 3 · Fold 4

X · H

Front spread · Back cover

W — W — W — W — W

H = Finished height
W = Finished width
X = Designer's choice

HOW TO FOLD

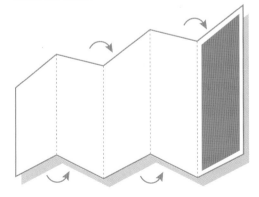
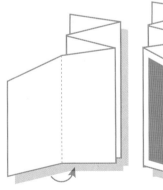
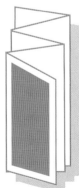

REVERSE ACCORDION FOLD

This folding style is great for smaller types of projects with light content. As much as the single-sidedness can be a benefit from a budget perspective, you do run the risk of the recipient overlooking any content that may be placed on the reverse side of the piece. To be safe, it is suggested that all critical content is placed on the front, and any support material, boilerplate information, or other less significant material is saved for the back.

DIRECT MAIL NOTE

Accordions are notoriously difficult for processes such as auto-insertion into envelopes and, if designed as a self-mailing piece, will require as many as four tabs to achieve mail-readiness. These issues will add to the production cost.

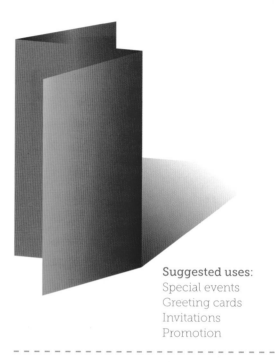

Suggested uses:
Special events
Greeting cards
Invitations
Promotion

The Reverse Accordion is a low budget champion. It is one of the very few folding styles that feature the cover and the interior spread on the same side of the sheet. What this means is that the designer has the option of printing on one side only. Of course, the reverse side of the folded piece offers a lot of real estate for additional material, but it would not look odd to leave it blank, as many choose to do.

PRODUCTION TIP

Accordions can be extended in length by adding more panels. If you are looking for more space for your layout, ask the printer if there is any extra room on the sheet to add another panel or two. If your budget is really tight, ask if there is anything you can do from a sizing perspective to get as many units on the sheet as possible. Sometimes a subtle size adjustment can allow for another unit on the sheet, which can really add up.

DIGITAL DOCUMENT SIDE 1

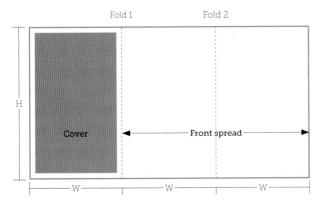

H = Finished height
W = Finished width

DIGITAL DOCUMENT SIDE 2

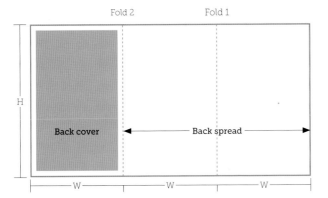

HOW TO FOLD

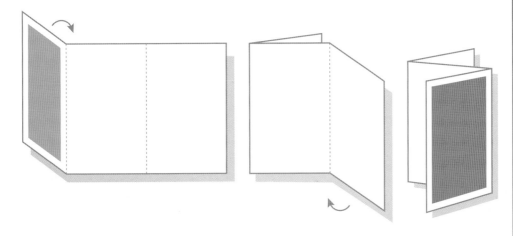

WRAPPED ACCORDION FOLD

Standard Accordion Folds are notoriously difficult for auto-insertion and require four tabs when produced as a self-mailing piece. What makes it so difficult to work with? Where many other folding styles such as Tri-Folds, Roll Folds, and Gate Folds fold into themselves to create a closed "package" of sorts, the Accordion folding style is very open in format, folding onto itself rather than into itself. The zig-zag technique creates open edges on either side, which allows it to expand with air and become difficult to insert and, from a mailing perspective, offers no closed edge for machinability at the post office. The solution is to add two tabs to each open edge to prevent the piece from expanding and jamming the machines.

By adding a cover to the Accordion Fold, you get the closed edge and an extra layer of protection to boot. Tabbing requirements are reduced and auto-insertion is no longer an issue.

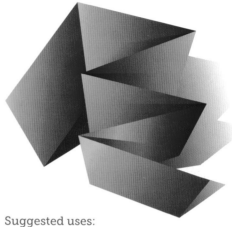

Suggested uses:
Promotion
Direct mail
Marketing collateral
Brochures

- -

This folding style is a practical solution in disguise. The Wrapped Accordion features the characteristic zig-zag Accordion experience, but with the extension of a cover and back cover that wrap around to enclose one of the edges. People are always surprised by the Wrapped Accordion, because the cover hides the fun, pull-out format.

FOLDING FACT
Technically there is no limit as to how many Accordion Folds you can create. However, anything above six folds becomes more difficult because most buckle plate folding machines have six plates that allow six folds in one direction. Once you exceed that number, the level of difficulty and production time (translation: cost) increases. At that point, the piece may need to be finished by hand. If you want a very long Accordion, your printer can create two long Accordion folded pieces and glue them together!

DIGITAL DOCUMENT SIDE 1

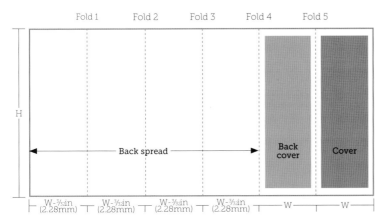

Fold 1   Fold 2   Fold 3   Fold 4   Fold 5

H

Back spread — Back cover — Cover

W-³⁄₃₂in (2.28mm)   W-³⁄₃₂in (2.28mm)   W-³⁄₃₂in (2.28mm)   W-³⁄₃₂in (2.28mm)   W   W

H = Finished height
W = Finished width

DIGITAL DOCUMENT SIDE 2

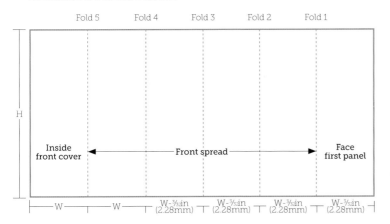

Fold 5   Fold 4   Fold 3   Fold 2   Fold 1

H

Inside front cover — Front spread — Face first panel

W   W   W-³⁄₃₂in (2.28mm)   W-³⁄₃₂in (2.28mm)   W-³⁄₃₂in (2.28mm)   W-³⁄₃₂in (2.28mm)

HOW TO FOLD

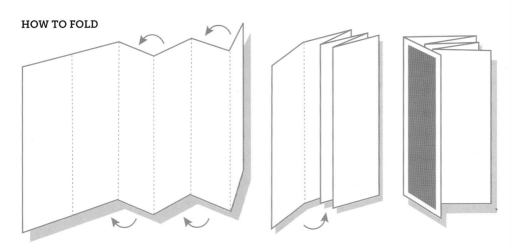

ACCORDION WITH FOLD-IN PANEL

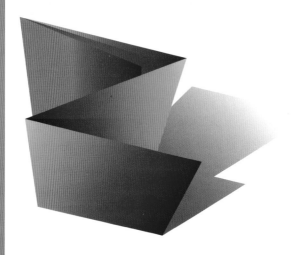

Suggested uses:
Marketing collateral
Brochures
Promotion

- -

The Accordion with Fold-in Panel zig-zags like a standard Accordion Fold, but the trailing panel reverses direction and folds inward. This style of folding is useful when you want to make the last panel a tear-off coupon, a business reply card (BRC), or simply as a little surprise at the end.

Paper choice is important for this folding style if you are planning to create a tear-off coupon or a BRC. Be sure that the sheet meets the necessary postal requirements for thickness (or for durability if it is a coupon), and that the dimension of the tear-off portion is compliant with the appropriate postal sizing specifications or envelope enclosure size.

DIRECT MAIL NOTE

Accordions are notoriously difficult for processes such as auto-insertion into envelopes and, if designed as a self-mailing piece, will require as many as four tabs to achieve mail-readiness. These issues will add to the production cost.

FLIP IT!

The fold-in panel can be an extension of the cover panel instead. As long as the fold-in panel is at one end or the other, it is the same folding style from your printer's perspective. However, the orientation of the graphics must be adjusted and, of course, the fold-in panel must be slightly shorter to account for the dimensionality of the sheet.

DIGITAL DOCUMENT SIDE 1

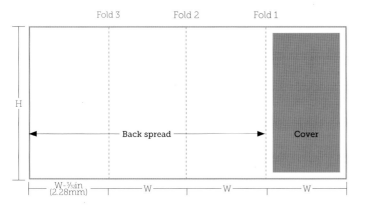

Fold 3   Fold 2   Fold 1

H

Back spread   Cover

W-⅜in
(2.28mm)   W   W   W

H = Finished height
W = Finished width

DIGITAL DOCUMENT SIDE 2

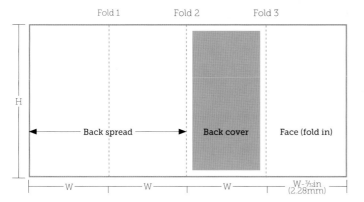

Fold 1   Fold 2   Fold 3

H

Back spread   Back cover   Face (fold in)

W   W   W   W-⅜in
(2.28mm)

HOW TO FOLD

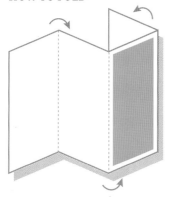
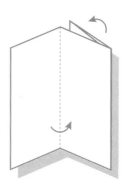

LETTER WITH SHORT COVER

The size of the short trim is up to the designer, and could be a slim pop of color on an edge or a wide and bold graphic callout.

Customers and clients will always open a bill or invoice and this folding style offers an easy way to get double duty out of your correspondence. This is also a digital print-friendly fold and can be greatly enhanced with the addition of variable data technology.

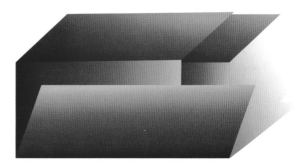

Suggested uses:
Letter mail
TransPromo
. Direct mail
Marketing collateral

- -

The Letter with Short Cover is a great way to get more mileage out of letter-format correspondence. The broadside format creates a lot of extra real estate for a marketing message, and the short trim on the cover offers a graphic sidebar to draw the viewer's attention and invite them to lift the cover to see more.

SIMPLIFY

Do you like this concept, but are not interested in sending a letter? Then do not Letter Fold it! Add pizzazz to a simple four-pager by trimming the cover short. It is cheap and easy, and you will get a lot of bang for your buck.

KNOW THE LINGO
What is TransPromo? TransPromo is the integration of relevant messages, promotional content, and advertising into transaction-related documents, such as bills, invoices, and statements.

DIGITAL DOCUMENT SIDE 1

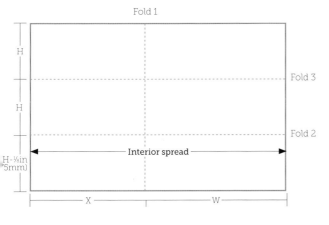

Fold 1

H

H

H-⅛in
(~5mm)

Back cover   Cover

Fold 3

Fold 2

W   X

DIGITAL DOCUMENT SIDE 2

Fold 1

H

H

H-⅛in
(~5mm)

◀——————— Interior spread ———————▶

Fold 3

Fold 2

X   W

H = Finished height
W = Finished width

HOW TO FOLD

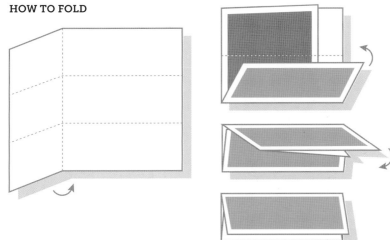

GATE FOLD

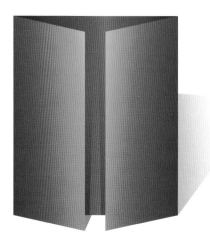

A Gate Fold involves two panels folding in toward the center to create the appearance of a gate. This folding style offers a nice reveal, and several opportunities to place critical marketing messages.

PRODUCTION TIP
Talk with your printer in advance about the desired gap or overlap of the fold-in panels. It is near-impossible to get the panels to meet exactly and touch, due to the likelihood of the panels nicking each other during the folding process. A plan implemented ahead of time ensures a good result.

Suggested uses:
Marketing collateral
Brochures
Events and invitations
Promotion
Direct mail

- -

There is an old rumor running around that Gate Folds are the most difficult and expensive folds to produce, generating lots of spoilage and requiring manual labor. The rumor has scared scores of designers into avoiding Gate Folds like the plague. The truth is, Gate Folds are actually not that big of a deal if your printer has the right equipment—and these days most of them do.

LEARNING THE LINGO
Many like to call this fold (and the Closed Gate Fold) a Double Gate. It is important to note that one panel folding in is not a Single Gate—there is no such thing as a Single Gate—and therefore two panels folding in is not a Double Gate. It is just a Gate.

DIGITAL DOCUMENT SIDE 1

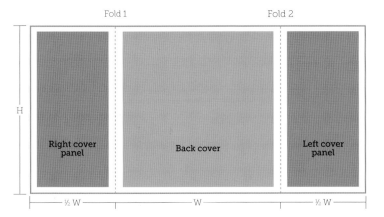

H = Finished height
W = Finished width

DIGITAL DOCUMENT SIDE 2

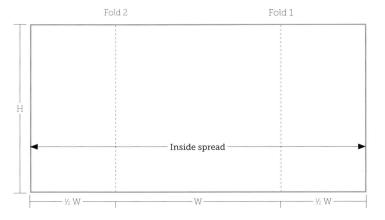

HOW TO FOLD

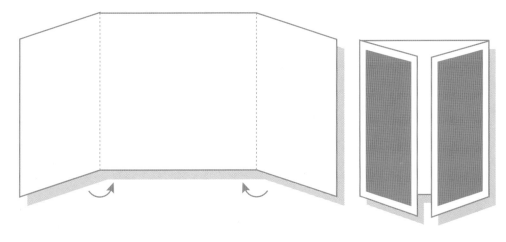

CLOSED GATE FOLD

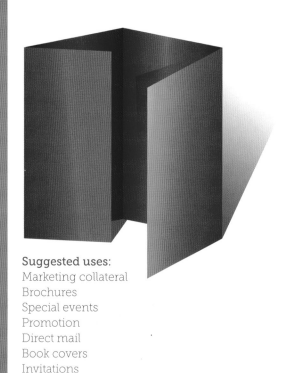

Suggested uses:
Marketing collateral
Brochures
Special events
Promotion
Direct mail
Book covers
Invitations

Closed Gates are quite possibly one of the most functional of all the folding styles. This fold can be dressed up for more formal content, or dressed down for day-to-day functional applications.

PRODUCTION TIP
Have you ever seen a Closed Gate Fold with a generous gap between the panels—the kind of gap that lets you see right through to the next spread? It is a designer's nightmare, and it is an example of what can happen if you leave it up to someone else to decide how much to trim the panels. Talk with your printer in advance about the desired trim on the fold-in panels if you want to ensure a tight gap.

The Closed Gate adds a third parallel fold to "close" the gate. Much friendlier for direct mail than the standard Gate, the Closed Gate offers a nice user experience and reveal, since the viewer will see an initial spread and then open the panels simultaneously to see a much larger spread.

MODIFICATION
The Closed Gate is commonly misidentified as a Double Gate. A true Double Gate Fold is gate-folded twice, so that the panels roll in toward the center from opposite directions. This folding style features a wide, six-panel interior and 12 pages, and is moderately difficult to produce.

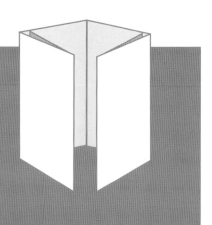

DIGITAL DOCUMENT SIDE 1

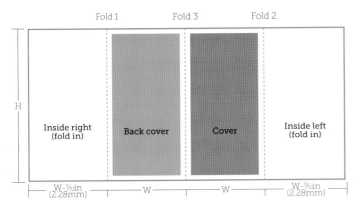

Fold 1   Fold 3   Fold 2

H

| Inside right (fold in) | Back cover | Cover | Inside left (fold in) |

W-³⁄₃₂in (2.28mm) — W — W — W-³⁄₃₂in (2.28mm)

H = Finished height
W = Finished width

DIGITAL DOCUMENT SIDE 2

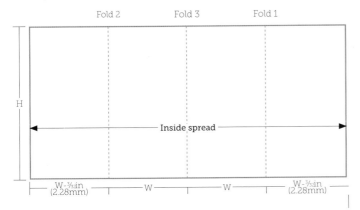

Fold 2   Fold 3   Fold 1

H

◄———————— Inside spread ————————►

W-³⁄₃₂in (2.28mm) — W — W — W-³⁄₃₂in (2.28mm)

HOW TO FOLD

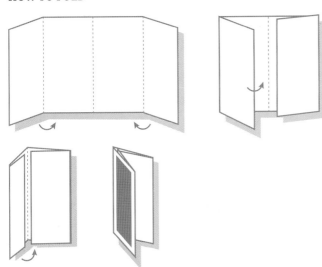

OPEN GATE FOLD

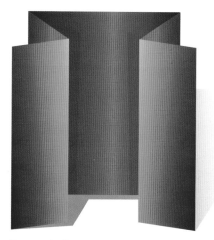

Suggested uses:
Special events
Invitations
Specialty/novelty projects
Promotion

This is an unusual fold that offers a lot of creative potential. For fun, the gate panels can be shorter to leave a gap in the middle, or longer to meet at the center. Left and right end panels can also be long or short to express a variety of different visual statements. Some printers will fold this style by hand, some by machine.

To maximize the structural quality of the Open Gate, the decision of paper weight is an important one. For best results, ask a printer or paper representative for folding dummies in the weights you are considering. A quality scoring technique will also help this fold to maintain its shape both when folded down and while standing.

- -

The Open Gate is a Gate Fold with two panels that extend from the fold-in panels, change direction and fold outward. This style is dimensional and great for self-standing types of applications, but not ideal for auto-inserting into envelopes.

MODIFICATION

If you would like to increase the direct mail-friendliness of this piece by adding a closed edge, you can add one more parallel fold to create a 5-Parallel Open Gate. Doing this also increases the level of difficulty and most likely the production cost, so talk with your printer if budget is a concern.

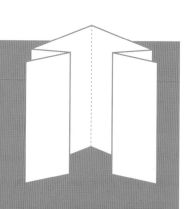

DIGITAL DOCUMENT SIDE 1

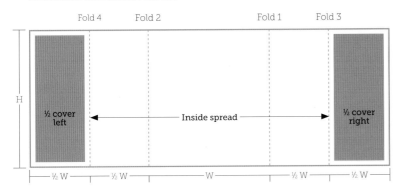

H = Finished height
W = Finished width

DIGITAL DOCUMENT SIDE 2

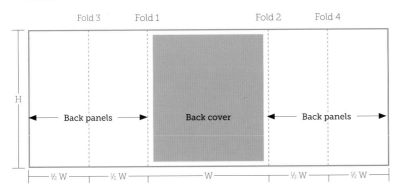

HOW TO FOLD

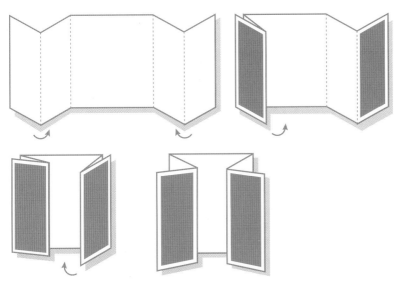

STEPPED DOUBLE PARALLEL FOLD

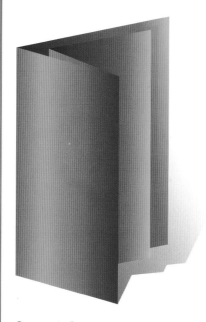

There is a lot of flexibility with regard to the depth of the steps, so play with the placement of the parallel folds. If you are just looking for texture or contrast, shallow steps may fit the bill; and if you are looking for tabs or large text running up the edge, wide steps will do the trick.

PAPER TIP

This folding style does not require a heavy sheet—choice of a sheet that is particularly bulky or rigid will result in the inability of the piece to lie flat and hold its shape. Ask for a paper dummy or sample sheets to play with to determine the best choice for your project.

Suggested uses:
Marketing collateral
Brochures
Tabbed content
Promotion

- -

The Stepped Double Parallel Fold is a fantastic update to an old standby. The traditional Double Parallel is folded in half and in half again. The stepped version is folded short of halfway, and then the cover folds short for a three-step profile.

CHEAP FOLD ALERT!

This fold consists of two simple Parallel Folds and is a great low budget solution. Try this fold the next time you have a moderate amount of content and multiple categories or sections to organize.

DIGITAL DOCUMENT SIDE 1

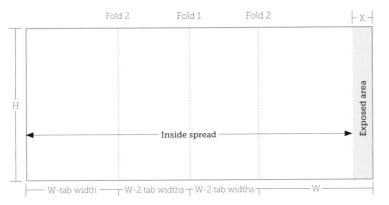

H = Finished height
W = Finished width
X = Designer's choice

DIGITAL DOCUMENT SIDE 2

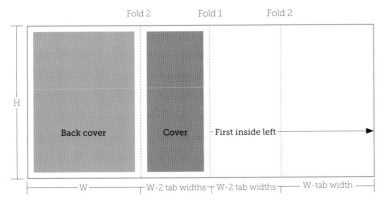

HOW TO FOLD

10-PAGE PARALLEL FOLD

One of the nice features of this folding style, from a design perspective, is the layered effect of the first fold-in panel opening to the two-panel spread, which ultimately reveals the four innermost concealed panels. Knowing this, the leftmost interior panel is very important, as it anchors all three of the described viewer experiences.

PAPER TIP
In most cases, this folding style should be produced on a text-weight sheet—choice of a sheet that is particularly bulky or rigid will result in the inability of the piece to lie flat and hold its shape. Ask for a paper dummy or sample sheets to play with to determine the best choice for your project.

Suggested uses:
Brochures
Promotion
Direct mail

The 10-Page Parallel Fold is made up of three parallel folds that together form a fold-in panel with two extra panels tucked in underneath for an interesting pull-out effect. This style is a good alternative to a Tri-Fold when you are looking for a similar format but are in need of a little more space for content.

DESIGNER'S TIP
Pay attention to the order of information. At a glance, this fold seems simple—and it is simple from a production standpoint. However, from the perspective of the placement of graphics, the order of reveal, and distribution of content, this style can be very complex. Make a mock-up and test your layout with a few colleagues to make sure they are reading it in the right order and receiving the critical marketing messages.

DIGITAL DOCUMENT SIDE 1

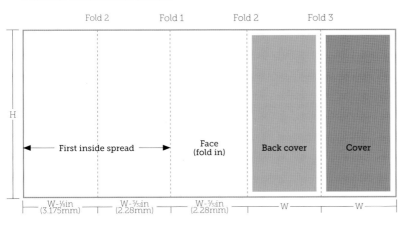

Fold 2   Fold 1   Fold 2   Fold 3

H

First inside spread →   Face (fold in)   Back cover   Cover

W-⅛in (3.175mm)   W-³⁄₃₂in (2.28mm)   W-³⁄₃₂in (2.28mm)   W   W

H = Finished height
W = Finished width

DIGITAL DOCUMENT SIDE 2

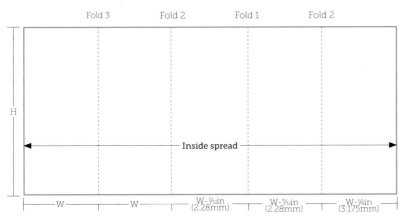

Fold 3   Fold 2   Fold 1   Fold 2

H

← Inside spread →

W   W   W-³⁄₃₂in (2.28mm)   W-³⁄₃₂in (2.28mm)   W-⅛in (3.175mm)

HOW TO FOLD

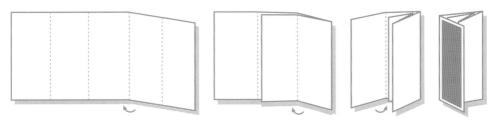

TRIPLE PARALLEL FOLD

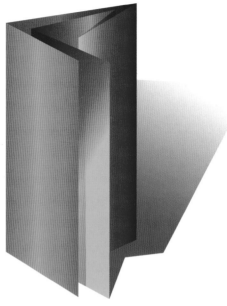

This folding style is especially useful for text-heavy projects, and for maps and other types of information graphics. It is common to see this folding style in literature holders at rest stops, as it is a very production-friendly format that can hold a lot of content. Unlike some other folds that may be considered for maps, this one feels at first like a Tri-Fold, and then opens to a spacious interior spread.

PAPER TIP

This folding style in most cases should be produced on a text-weight sheet—choice of a sheet that is particularly bulky or rigid will result in the inability of the piece to lie flat and hold its shape. Ask for a paper dummy or sample sheets to play with to determine the best choice for your project.

Suggested uses:
Maps/guides
Brochures
Promotion

- -

The Triple Parallel Fold consists of three parallel folds that together create a fold-in panel revealing three nested inner panels. The effect of this folding style is a long, pull-out six-panel interior spread.

FOLDING FACT

The Triple Parallel Fold can be confusing to fold back to its original state. Often the viewer will open the piece quickly, examine the contents, and then forget how it folded in the first place. This problem is not unique to this particular folding style—just about any time there is a large foldout spread, there can be confusion.

DIGITAL DOCUMENT SIDE 1

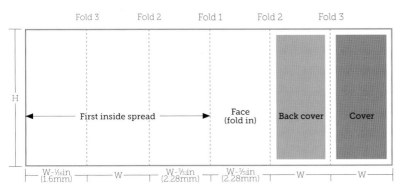

Fold 3   Fold 2   Fold 1   Fold 2   Fold 3

First inside spread → | Face (fold in) | Back cover | Cover

H

W-¹⁄₁₆in (1.6mm) — W — W-³⁄₃₂in (2.28mm) — W-³⁄₃₂in (2.28mm) — W — W

H = Finished height
W = Finished width

DIGITAL DOCUMENT SIDE 2

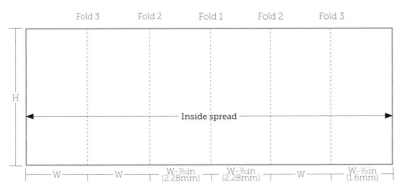

Fold 3   Fold 2   Fold 1   Fold 2   Fold 3

H

← Inside spread →

W — W — W-³⁄₃₂in (2.28mm) — W-³⁄₃₂in (2.28mm) — W — W-¹⁄₁₆in (1.6mm)

HOW TO FOLD

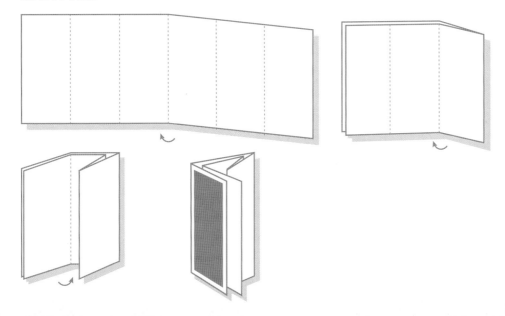

ASYMMETRICAL TRIPLE PARALLEL FOLD

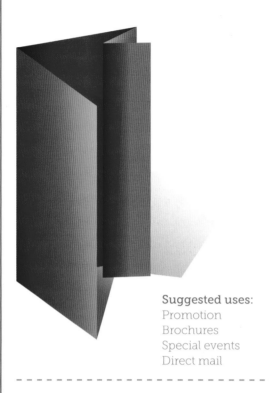

There is no rule as to what the lengths of the short panels must be, and those panels do not have to be the same size either. It could be very interesting to make one wider and one narrower for a stepped effect. The short panels provide a focal point for a callout quote, for the unique treatment of an image, or for a critical marketing message.

Suggested uses:
Promotion
Brochures
Special events
Direct mail

FOLDING TIP
Often when we fold, we create the appearance of symmetry, but asymmetry is a great technique for changing things from a folding perspective. And it is not just for this folding style. What if you took a Gate Fold and pushed the gap between the fold-in panels to off-center? Fresh! Consult a printer early on as you are exploring unconventional formats and techniques.

The Asymmetrical Triple Parallel Fold utilizes the unusual placement of three parallel folds to create a short pull-out section. This folding style is quite simple, and is a great example of the creative potential of using fold placement as a way to add interest to a folded piece.

DESIGNER'S TIP
Need help deciding which folding style to use? Consider folding as a technique for leading the viewer around the piece. How will you get their attention? How do you want them to experience the content? Do they need to read the content from start to finish? Is the information in short nuggets that they can read in any order? Do you want to surprise them, help them, educate them, amuse them, or provoke an action? If you understand the content you are designing for, and the desired response, it should help narrow down your selection.

DIGITAL DOCUMENT SIDE 1

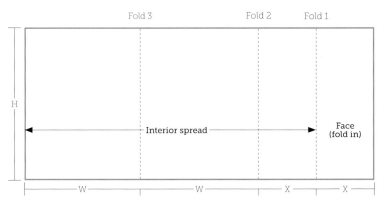

H = Finished height
W = Finished width
X = Designer's choice

DIGITAL DOCUMENT SIDE 2

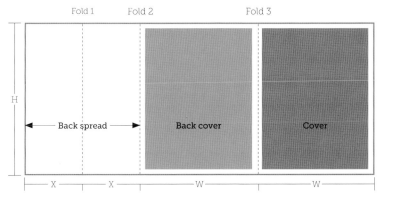

HOW TO FOLD

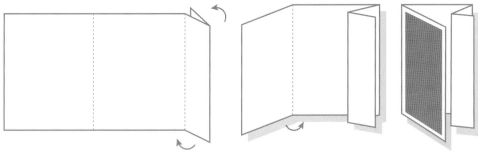

ROLL FOLD

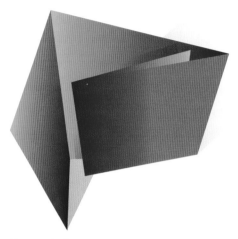

Roll Folds have a very natural opening sequence, and often the viewer rolls the piece out immediately, rather than stopping to view each panel as it is revealed. This should be a consideration when designing and placing text, as critical content may be overlooked.

ROLL FOLD FACT
Unlike Accordion Folds that can have infinite panels if glued together by hand, Roll Folds have considerable flexibility in panel count, but they do have their limitations. Roll Folds can have up to 15 panels, however Roll Folds with more than five panels are considered difficult or even specialty folds. Consult a printer before you consider increasing panel count, as fold placement, paper choice, and budget will become a factor.

Suggested uses:
Promotion
Brochures
Marketing collateral
Direct mail

The Roll Fold is characterized by a series of four or more panels that fold, or "roll," in on each other. The trick to a proper Roll Fold is that the panels must get increasingly smaller to accommodate for the dimensionality of the sheet, so fold placement and margins must be adjusted accordingly.

MODIFICATION
Sometimes all it takes is a change in direction to make your folded project feel fresh. If you like the Roll Fold, try a Vertical Roll! The Vertical Roll folds down instead of out to the right, taking the form of a tall vertical format. This fold is particularly effective when the intent is to reveal a large image or poster solution.

DIGITAL DOCUMENT SIDE 1

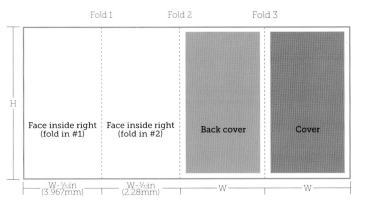

Fold 1   Fold 2   Fold 3

| Face inside right (fold in #1) | Face inside right (fold in #2) | Back cover | Cover |

H

W-⁵⁄₃₂in (3.967mm)   W-³⁄₃₂in (2.28mm)   W   W

H = Finished height
W = Finished width

DIGITAL DOCUMENT SIDE 2

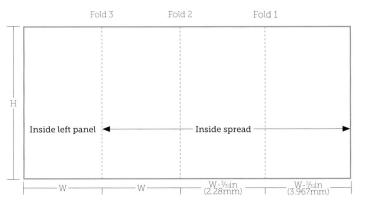

Fold 3   Fold 2   Fold 1

H

Inside left panel ◄————— Inside spread —————►

W   W   W-³⁄₃₂in (2.28mm)   W-⁵⁄₃₂in (3.967mm)

HOW TO FOLD

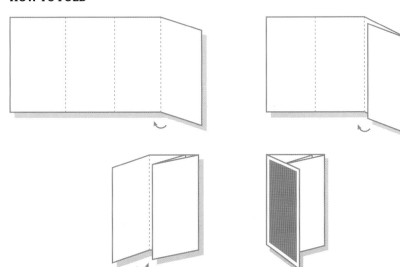

2-PIECE FAKE IRON CROSS FOLD

The standard Iron Cross is a notorious space hog. Its plus-shape does not allow for the nesting of more than one piece per sheet in most cases, which leads to a lot of waste and ultimately twice the amount of paper. Designers tend to use Iron Crosses for special projects—projects in which they might have the desire to use a particularly unusual sheet. "Unusual" tends to mean "expensive" so the ability to reduce the paper cost can make the difference between getting your Iron Cross Fold or choosing a different folding style that is more efficient on the sheet.

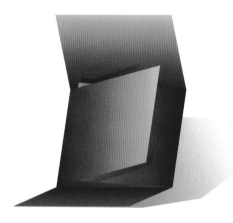

Suggested uses:
Special events
Invitations
Direct mail
Promotion
Specialty/novelty projects
Carrier

- -

This folding style is on the high end of moderate pricing, but the 2-Piece Fake Iron Cross is a space-saving alternative to the Iron Cross Specialty Fold (featured on pages 130–131). By creating two long rectangles, scoring, trimming, and gluing them together, you can achieve the same look while getting more than one-up on a sheet.

DIRECT MAIL TIP
It is common to see the Iron Cross built as a square-format piece, but square-format mail bears a massive financial surcharge for non-machinability. Iron Crosses can be rectangular, so experiment to find a format that qualifies for an economical postal rate and save yourself (or your client) some serious cash!

DIGITAL DOCUMENT SIDE 1

Fold 4   Fold 3

Inside left	Inside center	Inside right

H-¹⁄₁₆in (6mm)

├── W ──┤── W ──┤ W-³⁄₃₂in (2.28mm) ┤

Fold 3   Fold 4

Face (fold in)	Glue panel (not visible)	Cover

H-¹⁄₁₆in (5mm)

├ W-³⁄₃₂in (2.28mm) ┤── W ──┤── W ──┤

DIGITAL DOCUMENT SIDE 2

H-¹⁄₁₆in (1.6mm)

| Inside top |
| Glue panel (not visible) |
| Inside bottom |

H-¹⁄₁₆in (3.175mm)

Fold 1
Fold 2

H

├── W-¹⁄₁₆" (1.6mm) ──┤

H-¹⁄₁₆in (1.6mm)

| Inside top (rotate art 180°) |
| Back cover |
| Inside bottom (rotate art 180°) |

H-¹⁄₁₆in (3.175mm)

Fold 1
Fold 2

H

├── W-¹⁄₁₆in (1.6mm) ──┤

HOW TO FOLD

Align and glue together

H = Finished height
W = Finished width

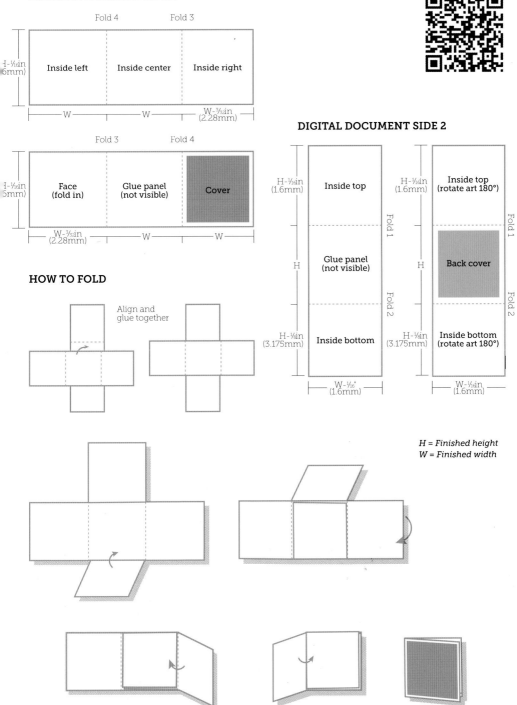

GALLERY

Stepped Double Parallel
design and illustration
by Kelsey Grafton

Vertical-format Wrapped
Accordion produced by
Specialties Graphic Finishers

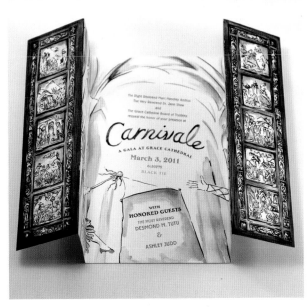

Upright-format Open Gate
Fold design and illustration
by Molly McCoy

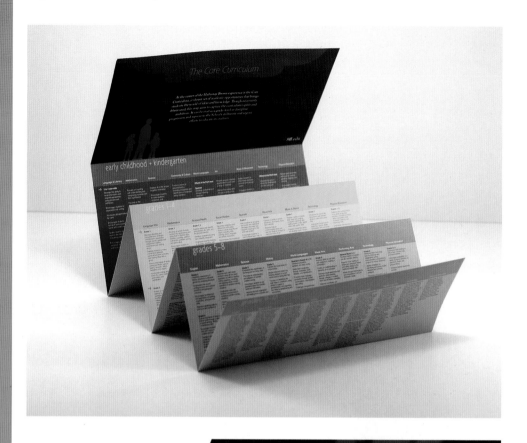

Vertical-format Wrapped Stepped Accordion produced by Chartreuse and Oliver Printing Co.

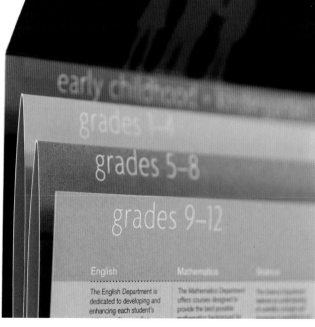

Tri-Fold with nested 8-page
short fold by Kanella Arapoglou
(left and below)

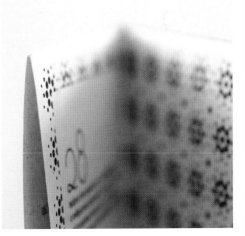

Tri-fold with short trim cover
and half-circle die-cut tab
produced by ColorCraft of
Virginia **(above and right)**

CHAPTER FOUR: FOLDING SPLURGES

Every now and again an opportunity presents itself—the right concept, the right budget, and the right client intersect and magic can happen. It is a great position to be in, but it can also be overwhelming. When anything is possible, nothing is ruled out and it can be difficult to make a choice, or to feel as though you have seen enough options.

Exotic folding styles are fun and can be a fabulous way to grab the attention of your viewer—but choose wisely. An exciting fold can confuse or distract as much as it can captivate. Success relies on the proper choice of fold, distribution of content, paper choice, and placement of critical marketing messages. The best folded print materials utilize folding as a component of the overall design concept and delivery, and not as a gimmick.

All things considered, you are a lucky duck, so take your time and explore—and do not forget to have fun in the process. The folding samples in this chapter are all in the moderate-to-high production price range. These designs are really just the tip of the iceberg and can be modified into a world of interesting configurations. For best results, enlist the guidance of an experienced print professional at an early stage in the process.

Note

Many of the folding styles in this section would generally be folded by hand. But it is important to note that just about any folded solution, no matter how unusual, can be finished by machine if the quantity is high enough. If you produce print materials in high quantities, you may be surprised at the kinds of folding solutions that can be automated at a specialty bindery. Specialty binderies can engineer their machines to suit unconventional configurations—do a little research or ask your printer to help you locate one.

TIP

Your goal should be to provoke a response, not to end up in someone's "cool ideas" folder. Print out and mock-up your folded piece and hand it to several people, watching them react to it—note facial expressions, order of opening, etc.—and then take it out of their hands and ask them what the message was, or what action the piece wants them to take. If they did not get the message, re-work your content or you could waste a lot of money on a stylish but ineffective solution.

STEPPED ACCORDION FOLD

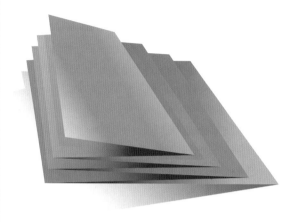

The panels of this particular variation of Stepped Accordion taper in pairs. Most designers choose either ¼in (6.35mm) or ½in (12.7mm) tabs; however, there is no rule regarding tab depth or panel count. Stepped Accordions offer a built-in organizational structure that can be really helpful when you have content that is written in distinct categories or sections.

Suggested uses:

Tabbed content
Brochures
Promotion
Marketing collateral

PRODUCTION NOTE

This fold can be produced by machine, but the set-up can be long and challenging. Depending upon the run length of the job, some printers will choose to fold the Stepped Accordion by hand.

- -

The Stepped Accordion features the zig-zag format of an Accordion Fold, but with panels that taper to create a stepped effect along the right edge. There are many variations on the Stepped Accordion, and the key to identifying a basic one is the existence of a flush edge on one side and a stepped edge on the other.

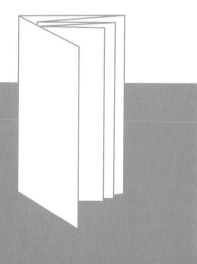

DIRECT MAIL MODIFICATION

Stepped Accordions are problematic as self-mailers, due to the fact that they have an open edge on one side and the stepped edge on the other. Make the fold direct mail-friendly by adding a wrap cover! The Wrapped Stepped Accordion adds a cover and closes an edge, making it a smart and interesting choice for direct mail.

DIGITAL DOCUMENT SIDE 1

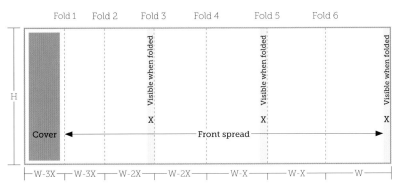

Fold 1   Fold 2   Fold 3   Fold 4   Fold 5   Fold 6

H

Cover

Visible when folded   X

Visible when folded   X

Visible when folded   X

Front spread

W-3X — W-3X — W-2X — W-2X — W-X — W-X — W

H = Finished height
W = Finished width
X = Tab depth

DIGITAL DOCUMENT SIDE 2

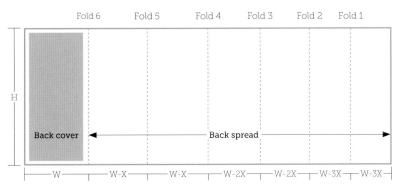

Fold 6   Fold 5   Fold 4   Fold 3   Fold 2   Fold 1

H

Back cover

Back spread

W — W-X — W-X — W-2X — W-2X — W-3X — W-3X

HOW TO FOLD

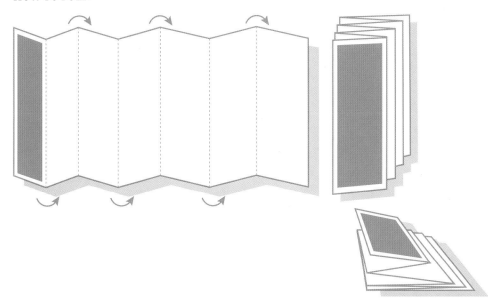

CENTERED STEPPED ACCORDION FOLD

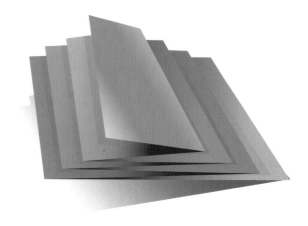

Unlike the standard Stepped Accordion where the panels taper in pairs, the panels of the Centered Stepped Accordion must taper consecutively, each smaller than the previous by the measurement of the tab depth. Most designers choose either ¼in (6.35mm) or ½in (12.7mm) tabs; however, there is no rule regarding tab depth or panel count. This folding style is great if the content for your folded project is in many categories, as it generates double the tabs of a standard Stepped Accordion Fold.

Get organized! A poorly organized Stepped Accordion can be a confusing mess. Make sure it is clear to the recipient what content relates to which tab, and use visual aids such as color and graphic symbols to clarify the message.

PRODUCTION NOTE

This is a difficult folding style to produce, and many printers will fold by hand to avoid the makeready; however, this can be automated.

Suggested uses:
Tabbed content
Brochures
Promotion
Marketing collateral

- -

The Centered Stepped Accordion features the zig-zag format of an Accordion Fold, and the tapered characteristics of a Stepped Accordion Fold, but with panels that taper toward the center to create a stepped effect along both the right and left edges.

DESIGNER'S TIP
Do not let yourself get overzealous with the tabs. If there are too many panels, and ultimately too many tabs, the piece can go from clever and convenient to cumbersome and confusing.

DIGITAL DOCUMENT SIDE 1

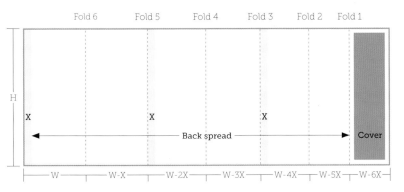

Fold 6   Fold 5   Fold 4   Fold 3   Fold 2   Fold 1

H

X   X   X

◄──────────── Back spread ────────────► Cover

├─ W ─┼─ W-X ─┼─ W-2X ─┼─ W-3X ─┼─ W-4X ─┼─ W-5X ─┼─ W-6X ─┤

H = Finished height
W = Finished width
X = Tab depth

DIGITAL DOCUMENT SIDE 2

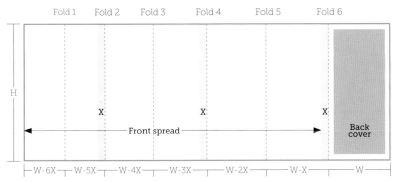

Fold 1   Fold 2   Fold 3   Fold 4   Fold 5   Fold 6

H

X   X   X

◄──────────── Front spread ────────────► Back cover

├─ W-6X ─┼─ W-5X ─┼─ W-4X ─┼─ W-3X ─┼─ W-2X ─┼─ W-X ─┼─ W ─┤

HOW TO FOLD

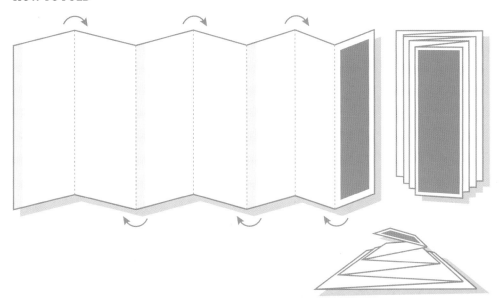

BIDIRECTIONAL ACCORDION FOLD

This style is very unusual and creates a wonderful feeling of discovery when opened. It is best to feature strong visuals in the shorter reveal sections that flow through the center, rather than critical content that must be read, since the natural pull of the horizontal folds will entice the viewer to allow it to fold back into place.

Paper choice is critical for the Bidirectional Accordion. A sheet that is too heavy will be problematic for right-angle folding and may cause wrinkling and bulkiness at the corner joints of the folds. A sheet that is too light will not adequately conceal the added thickness of the folds along the center, and can be prone to distracting impression marks. Work with your printer or paper representative to determine the best solution.

Most printers will choose to score and fold this style by hand; however, it is possible to automate this fold.

Suggested uses:
Special events
Maps/guides
Promotion
Marketing collateral

The Bidirectional Accordion features a long, two-parallel Accordion Fold on the horizontal, then changes direction and right-angle accordion folds down to finished size.

DESIGNER'S TIP
This folding style works better with fewer Accordion panels. The more panels this folding style has, the harder it is to lift up the Accordion that runs through the center.

DIGITAL DOCUMENT SIDE 1

Fold 4   Fold 3

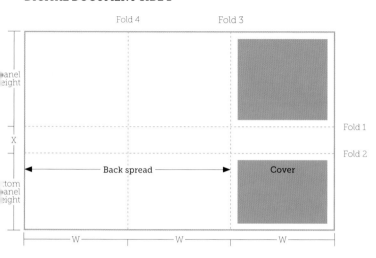

Panel
height

X

Bottom
panel
height

Fold 1

Fold 2

Back spread   Cover

W   W   W

H = Finished height
W = Finished width
X = Designer's choice

DIGITAL DOCUMENT SIDE 2

Fold 3   Fold 4

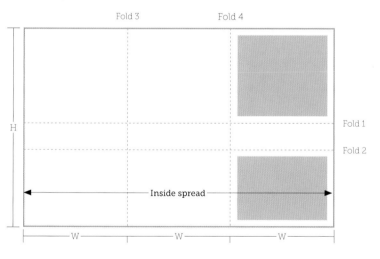

H

Fold 1

Fold 2

Inside spread

W   W   W

HOW TO FOLD

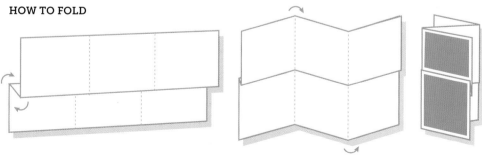

ASYMMETRICAL ACCORDION FOLD

There is a lot of opportunity with this style from a creative standpoint. You can use the shorter panels to artfully crop or split images, or to feature a special callout or other important piece of information. The result is visual and sculptural, and the recipient is likely to be tempted to display the piece because of its uniqueness.

Paper choice is important. As with any of the more sculptural folding styles, a bit of stiffness in the sheet can give it the stability it needs. Create a few paper dummies to test the overall experience of the folded piece.

This folding style requires scoring and total or partial handwork.

Suggested uses:
Promotion
Special events
Invitations
Specialty/novelty projects

- -

The Asymmetrical Accordion offers an interesting visual experience through the varied lengths of its Accordion panels. There are no rules for this style, but the key to success is to shorten the panels in pairs—otherwise, the piece will not finish flush.

DESIGNER'S TIP
Do not get cute. It may be tempting to make lots of short panels sandwiched between longer end panels, but the result can be flimsy and awkward. Place your shorter panels strategically and sparingly.

DIGITAL DOCUMENT SIDE 1

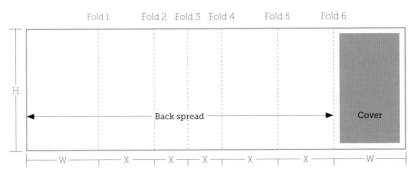

H = Finished height
W = Finished width
X = Designer's choice

There is no formula behind asymmetrical accordion panel measurements. Set-up is entirely up to the designer. For best results, shorten panels in pairs to assure the covers finish flush.

DIGITAL DOCUMENT SIDE 2

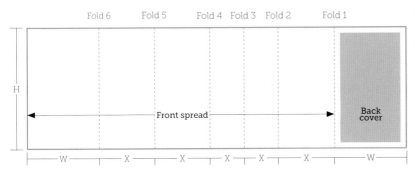

HOW TO FOLD

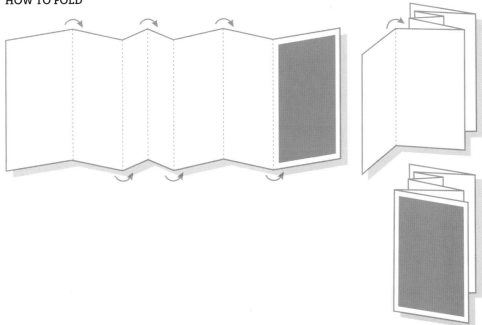

POP-OUT ACCORDION FOLD

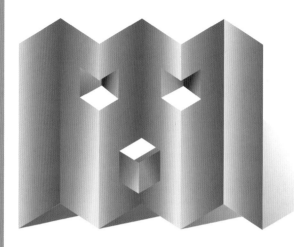

These are really fun to create, and a great way to work with the zig-zag nature of the Accordion. It is also important to note that there are different configurations for the pop boxes. You can get creative, connecting and stacking them like a pyramid. You can also choose to be selective—there is no rule that there must be a pop box on every fold or in certain places.

This folding style requires a heavier sheet for structure, scoring, die-cutting, and some handwork. When the boxes are "popped" this piece can get very thick, so if you are sending it through the mail, be sure it fits in the envelope and does not exceed thickness requirements. It is not unusual for the boxes to be left flat; however, this assumes the recipient will know how to pop them.

Suggested uses:
Promotion
Special events
Greeting cards
Invitations
Specialty/novelty projects

- -

The Pop-out Accordion is an Accordion Fold enhanced by the addition of short scores and die-cuts across the fold that enable dimensional shapes to pop out against the direction of the folds.

MODIFICATION
Pop-outs are not just for Accordion Folds. If you have a fold, you can work against the direction of that fold. For example, create a pop box on the innermost fold of a Roll Fold. When you lift the cover, there will be a square "window" on the left edge of the fold-in panel, and when you open the panels, a dimensional box will pop up! Don't like the window? Create a Broadside Fold and cut the pop boxes into the interior spread—it will be fun to decide what color or imagery will show through behind the pop boxes.

DIGITAL DOCUMENT SIDE 1

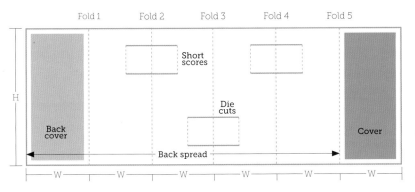

Fold 1 Fold 2 Fold 3 Fold 4 Fold 5

H

Back cover

Short scores

Die cuts

Cover

Back spread

W — W — W — W — W — W

H = *Finished height*
W = *Finished width*

Boxes can be placed anywhere and in any configuration. There is no particular rule for placement.

DIGITAL DOCUMENT SIDE 2

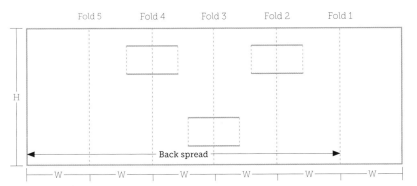

Fold 5 Fold 4 Fold 3 Fold 2 Fold 1

H

Back spread

W — W — W — W — W — W

HOW TO FOLD

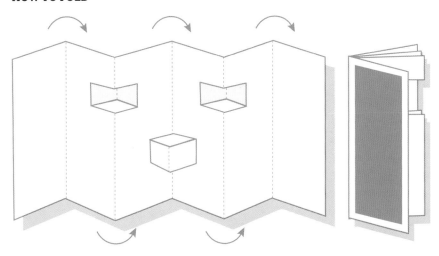

MEANDERING ACCORDION FOLD

This folding style has the characteristic zig-zag format of the accordion fold family. Its uniqueness is in the connected trailing panels that hinge and flip the piece, taking it into the opposite direction. There are not many limits to this folding style, as it can begin with as few or as many panels as desired, and can change direction limitless times as well. The decision to be made is, at what point does the piece turn 180 degrees and start heading in the opposite direction?

Paper choice is important with this fold. Any time there is an unexpected element in a fold, you have a risk of the recipient not doing what they're supposed to do. In this case, if the recipient doesn't realize the piece turns, they may tear the piece at the joint if the paper is too light. Make a few paper dummies in different weights to determine the best choice for feel and durability.

The Meandering Accordion requires scoring, die-cutting, and hand folding. Consult a printer in the early planning stages for best results, as this is a very unusual format.

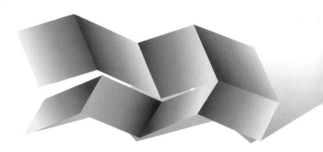

Suggested uses:
Special events
Specialty/novelty projects
Promotion
Direct mail
Marketing materials

- -

The Meandering Accordion has the initial appearance of a standard Accordion Fold, but once the viewer starts to experience the piece, an exciting twist is discovered.

DESIGNER'S TIP

This folding style is a lot of fun to work with, but it can also become unwieldy and difficult for the recipient to manage if it makes a lot of twists and turns. This is not a good choice for text-heavy content, or for anything that must be read in a specific order or referenced easily and often.

DIGITAL DOCUMENT SIDE 1

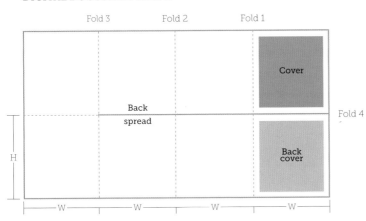

Fold 3 | Fold 2 | Fold 1

Cover

Back spread

Fold 4

Back cover

H

W — W — W — W

H = Finished height
W = Finished width

DIGITAL DOCUMENT SIDE 2

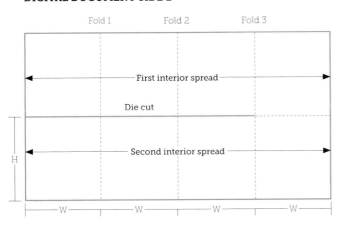

Fold 1 | Fold 2 | Fold 3

First interior spread

Die cut

Second interior spread

H

W — W — W — W

HOW TO FOLD

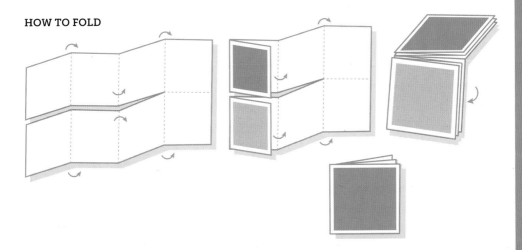

SWINGER FOLD

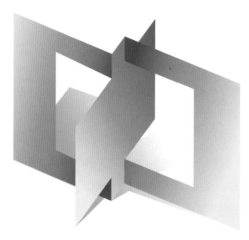

The only way for this fold to work as it is supposed to, is to use short scores at the folds above and below the swinging center panel. The length of the scores should not be less than ¾in (19mm). There are a lot of creative options for the swinging panel; the die-cut can be basic and square or an unusual shape.

This folding style works best with a heavier sheet for structural stability, and requires scoring, die-cutting, and can be left flat or hand-folded.

Suggested uses:
Promotion
Special events
Greeting cards
Invitations
Specialty/novelty projects

The Swinger Fold modifies a Short Accordion panel with die-cutting and scoring to create a swinging center panel. This folding style can create a real surprise for the recipient. If left flat, it can look like a simple postcard, but when picked up, the scores help to set the fold in motion and the center swings and flips over.

MODIFICATION
Working from a similar principle, a die-cut shape can extend from one panel into the next to create a swinging shape. The trick is to score at the fold up to the edge of the shape, being careful not to score through it, then die-cut around the shape and back to the fold, and finally continue the score to the length of the fold. Want a real challenge? Try this technique on a Stepped Accordion, extending a shape-off of each tab.

DIGITAL DOCUMENT SIDE 1

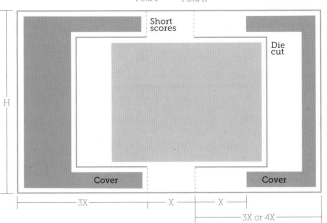

Fold 1   Fold 2

Short scores

Die cut

Cover   Cover

H

3X   X   X

3X or 4X

H = Finished height
X = Designer's choice

There is no particular rule regarding the shape of the die, or the size or placement of it. This diagram illustrates the basic principle only.

DIGITAL DOCUMENT SIDE 2

Fold 2   Fold 1

H

Back

3X or 4X   X   3X

HOW TO FOLD

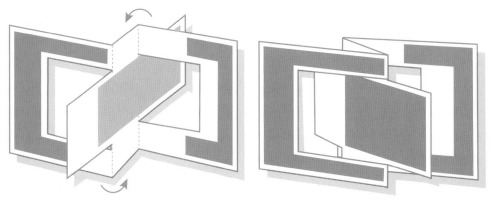

CORNER FOLDER

This folding style makes for a nice "package." Design square or fancy-shaped inserts to be placed inside and seal with a tab. Ensure the dimensions of the insert are at least ⅛in (3.17mm) smaller than the finished dimension of the piece. The inserts will have to be hand inserted, which will add to the production cost, and bear in mind that the square format will require extra postage if mailed.

This is an unusual folding style, so be sure to send a folding dummy to the printer in the early stages of the job. This will allow them to get familiar with it and to make any necessary adjustments to the die. The Corner Folder requires scoring and hand-folding, unless it is sent to a specialty bindery that can automate the folding process.

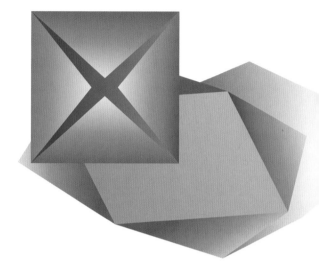

Suggested uses:
Promotion
Special events
Invitations
Specialty/novelty projects
Carrier

- -

The Corner Folder is a Specialty Fold in which the four corners of a square-trimmed sheet fold in to meet at the center. The result is a dynamic, square format piece that entices the viewer to open it.

DIRECT-MAIL MODIFICATION
Love the corner folder, but hate the cost of square-format mail? Make the Corner Folder mail-friendly with the addition of a horizontal fold at vertical center. The fold will create a closed edge and will turn the piece from square to rectangular, allowing for machinable rates (as long as the finished product is within letter size constraints and aspect ratio). The addition of the final fold in half greatly increases the difficulty of the fold. This modification may require the services of a specialty bindery.

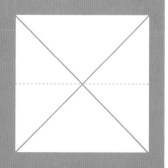

DIGITAL DOCUMENT SIDE 1

DIGITAL DOCUMENT SIDE 2

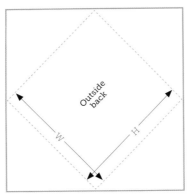

H = Finished height
W = Finished width

HOW TO FOLD

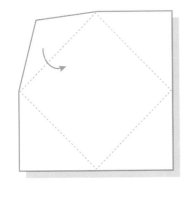

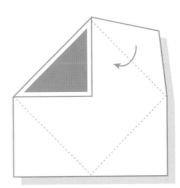

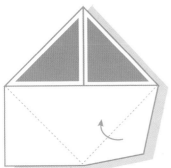

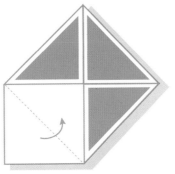

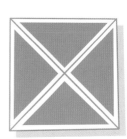

LAYERED CORNER FOLDER

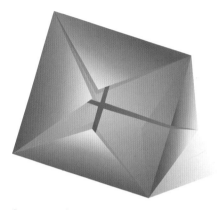

Suggested uses:
Promotion
Special events
Invitations
Specialty/novelty projects

- -

The Layered Corner Folder is like the standard Corner Folder in that the four corners of a square-trimmed sheet fold in to meet at the center; however, in the Layered Corner Folder the fold-in process is executed twice, or even thrice for a layered effect and an exciting and visual reveal of the interior contents.

This folding style is one of the more artful that exist, and you can see that it was influenced by origami. Paper choice is critical if the piece is to lay flat and avoid wrinkles, tearing, or bulkiness. A lightweight sheet is going to be the best choice, so experiment with a few weights and finishes to determine the look and feel you desire.

Bear in mind that the square format of this piece will require extra postage if mailed. The Layered Corner Folder requires scoring and hand-folding, a tab (unless inserted into an envelope), and careful paper selection.

STYLE MODIFICATION
This fold does not have to start as a square. For example, a rectangular sheet can be Gate-folded into a square, and then Corner-folded down to the final, smaller square format. It can take some experimentation and testing with your printer or paper representative, but there are many different approaches to this fold.

DIGITAL DOCUMENT SIDE 1

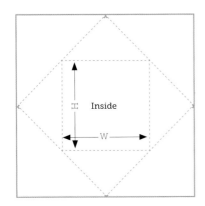

DIGITAL DOCUMENT SIDE 2

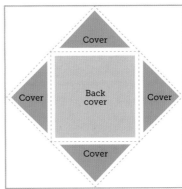

H = Finished height
W = Finished width

HOW TO FOLD

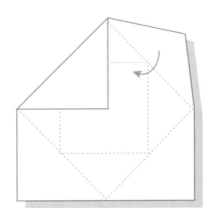

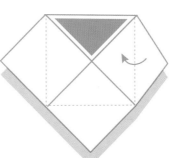

IRON CROSS FOLD

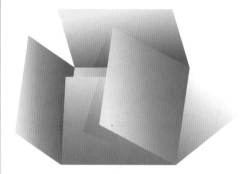

Iron Crosses are notorious for being space hogs on a press sheet. In most cases, the format of this fold allows for only one-up on a sheet, which leads to a lot of waste and increased paper cost. An alternative is to build a Fake Iron Cross (see pages 102–103) by creating two long rectangles and gluing them together—a configuration that will print two-up on a sheet.

This folding style makes for a nice "package." Design square or fancy-shaped inserts to be placed inside. Be sure the dimensions of the insert are at least ⅛in (3.17mm) smaller than the finished dimension of the piece. The inserts will have to be hand-inserted, which will add to the production cost. Iron Crosses do not have to finish as a square format, but this is the most common choice. Square-format mail forces a significant jump in postage costs, due to non-machinability. Iron Crosses require scoring, die-cutting, and can be folded by hand or by machine.

Suggested uses:
Promotion
Special events
Invitations
Specialty/novelty projects
Carrier

- -

The Iron Cross gets its name from the cross shape it creates when laid out flat. Panels can be added in any direction and can open in any sequence, but panel sizes must be adjusted based upon which panels will open first.

DESIGNER'S TIP
An Iron Cross Fold requires a custom die, so why not add to it? If it makes sense from a conceptual standpoint, consider adding die windows in different sizes on each of the four fold-in panels. When the piece is folded, the windows combine to create a layered shadowbox effect.

DIGITAL DOCUMENT SIDE 1

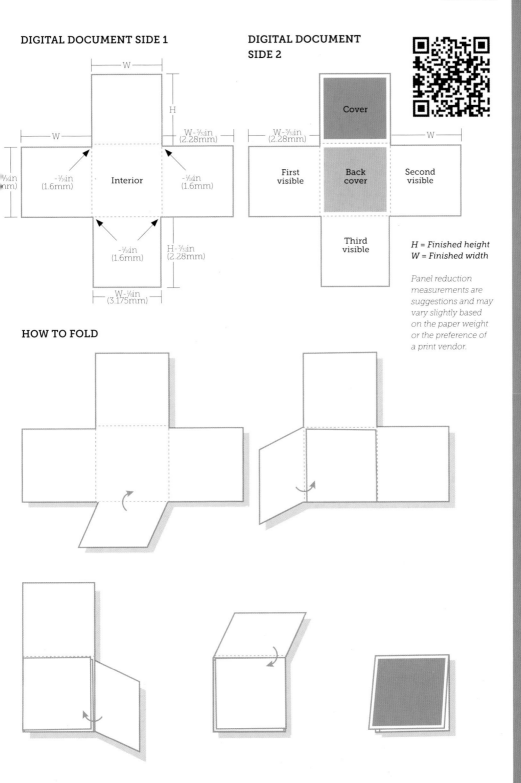

W

H

W

W-³⁄₃₂in
(2.28mm)

-¹⁄₁₆in
(1.6mm)

Interior

-¹⁄₁₆in
(1.6mm)

¹⁄₁₆in
(mm)

-¹⁄₁₆in
(1.6mm)

H-³⁄₃₂in
(2.28mm)

W-¹⁄₈in
(3.175mm)

DIGITAL DOCUMENT SIDE 2

Cover

W-³⁄₃₂in
(2.28mm)

W

First
visible

Back
cover

Second
visible

Third
visible

H = Finished height
W = Finished width

*Panel reduction
measurements are
suggestions and may
vary slightly based
on the paper weight
or the preference of
a print vendor.*

HOW TO FOLD

ROLLING IRON CROSS FOLD

This folding style can be very creative and fun to work with, but it exists by combining two of the most difficult folds into one. The standard Iron Cross is a production challenge, but add rolling panels that must get increasingly smaller to tuck into each other, and the math can get tough fast. Do not let the difficult set-up of this fold deter you if you really want to use it—just ask your printer involved at the earliest stages to get the details of the die sorted out in plenty of time.

Iron Crosses do not have to finish as a square format, but this is the most common choice for the style. Bear in mind that square-format mail forces a significant jump in postage costs, due to non-machinability. The Rolling Iron Cross requires scoring, die-cutting, and hand-folding.

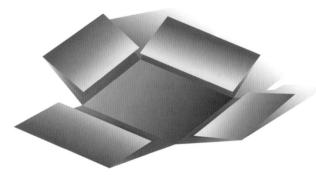

Suggested uses:
Promotion
Special events
Invitations
Specialty/novelty projects

- -

The Rolling Iron Cross holds the same plus-shape of a standard Iron Cross Fold, but with extra panels in one or multiple directions that roll in toward the center.

DESIGNER'S TIP
Consider asymmetry. Instead of adding an equal number of panels in every direction, try one very long rolling panel, or building on the panel count as the viewer opens the piece, with a single panel, then a double panel, then a triple panel, and then finally a quad. Experiment and have fun!

DIGITAL DOCUMENT SIDE 1

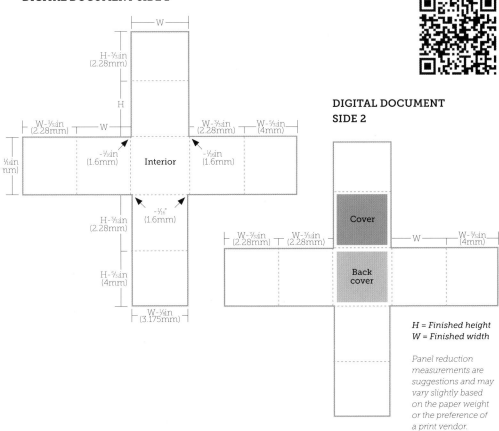

DIGITAL DOCUMENT SIDE 2

H = Finished height
W = Finished width

Panel reduction measurements are suggestions and may vary slightly based on the paper weight or the preference of a print vendor.

HOW TO FOLD

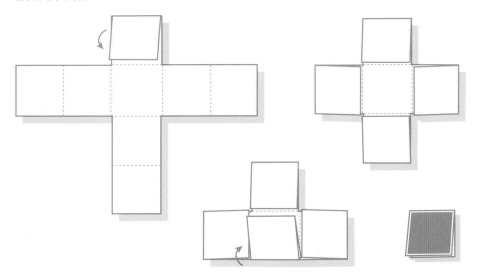

L-CROSS FOLD

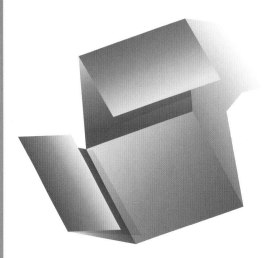

L-Crosses are uncommon, and can offer a unique presentation of written content and imagery. The simple shape of this folding style creates a path and a definitive direction of flow. In contrast, Iron Crosses offer content that fold out into four directions, which can be confusing at times for the viewer.

Extra panels can be added to both ends—you can even build an L-Cross that finishes with a Closed Gate Fold. Get your printer involved at an early stage for best results.

L-Crosses do not have to finish as a square format, but square format is the most common choice for this style. Square-format mail forces a significant jump in postage costs, due to non-machinability. The L-Cross requires scoring, die-cutting, and hand-folding.

Suggested uses:
Promotion
Special events
Invitations
Specialty/novelty projects

- -

The L-Cross is a relative of the Iron Cross Fold and gets its name from the "L" shape it creates when laid out flat. L-Cross Folds tend to nest better on a press sheet than Iron Crosses, which can make them a nice alternative.

DESIGNER'S TIP

L-Crosses are very unusual, and the process of unfolding one is not necessarily intuitive. Make sure the sheet is heavy enough to resist the minor stress that will almost inevitably occur in the unfolding process. The recipient may try to continue to unfold in one direction if they do not realize the direction of the fold just turned 90°. This action could cause an unsightly tear.

DIGITAL DOCUMENT SIDE 1

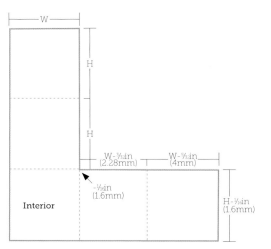

W-³⁄₃₂in
(2.28mm)

W-⁵⁄₃₂in
(4mm)

-¹⁄₁₆in
(1.6mm)

Interior

H-¹⁄₁₆in
(1.6mm)

DIGITAL DOCUMENT SIDE 2

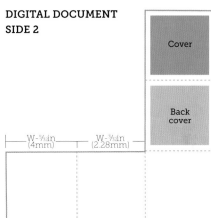

Cover

Back
cover

W-⁵⁄₃₂in
(4mm)

W-³⁄₃₂in
(2.28mm)

HOW TO FOLD

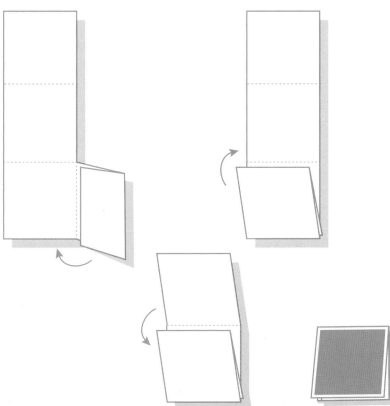

H = Finished height
W = Finished width

*Panel reduction
measurements are
suggestions and may
vary slightly based
on the paper weight
or the preference of
a print vendor.*

T-CROSS FOLD

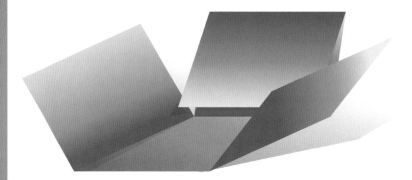

Suggested uses:
Promotion
Special events
Invitations
Specialty/novelty projects

- -

The T-Cross is a relative of the Iron Cross Fold and gets its name from the "T" shape it creates when laid out flat. Depending upon size and format choices, a T-Cross may be able to nest better on a press sheet than an Iron Cross, which could mean the difference between getting one-up and two-up on a sheet.

Unlike the Iron Cross, whose four fold-in panels create a closed interior space, the T-Cross is not a good "carrier" of materials, due to the open edge; however, materials could still be placed in that space (they just might not stay there).

T-Crosses do not have to finish as a square format, but this is the most common choice for the style. Square-format mail forces a significant jump in postage costs, due to non-machinability. The T-Cross requires scoring, die-cutting, and can be folded by hand or by machine.

DILEMMA
Why choose a T-shape over a plus-shape or an L-shape? The answer to that question is subjective, but it has everything to do with your concept and with the content you have to work with. An interesting shape means nothing if the viewer does not get it. Choose your folding configuration based upon the style and pacing of the content, and the order in which it must be read. Use folding to walk the reader through the content.

DIGITAL DOCUMENT SIDE 1

W — W — W-³⁄₃₂in (2.28mm)

H

Interior

H-³⁄₃₂in (2.28mm)

-¹⁄₁₆in (1.6mm)

H-⁵⁄₃₂in (4mm)

W-¹⁄₈in (3.175mm)

DIGITAL DOCUMENT SIDE 2

W-³⁄₃₂in (2.28mm) — W — W

Back cover

Cover

H = Finished height
W = Finished width

Panel reduction measurements are suggestions and may vary slightly based on the paper weight or the preference of a print vendor.

HOW TO FOLD

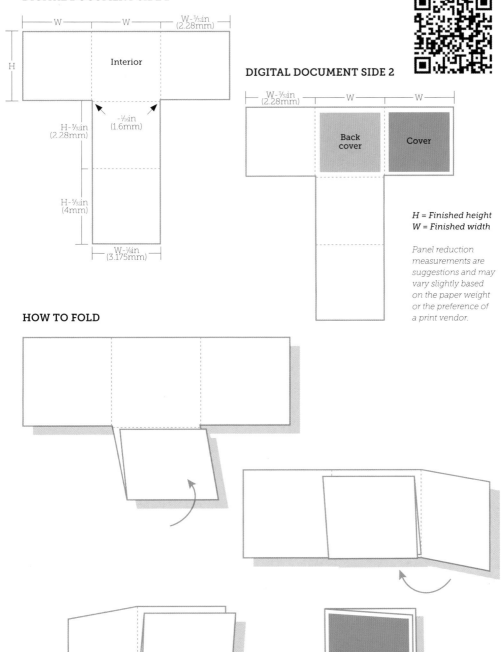

BOX TOP FOLD

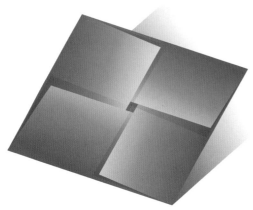

Suggested uses:
Promotion
Special events
Invitations
Specialty/novelty
projects
Carrier

The Box Top is configured like an Iron Cross Fold, except the panels are short, folding in to meet at the center. The last panel to fold in tucks under the first, like one would close the top of a cardboard box. The final tuck locks the piece closed, so you do not need a tab.

This folding style makes for a nice "package." Design square or fancy-shaped inserts to be placed inside. Be sure the dimensions of the insert are at least ⅛in (3.17mm) smaller than the finished dimension of the piece. The inserts will have to be hand-inserted, which will add to the production cost.

The Box Top does not have to finish as a square format, but square format is the most common choice for this style. Square-format mail forces a significant jump in postage costs, due to non-machinability. The Box Top requires scoring, die-cutting, and hand-folding.

DESIGNER'S TIP
This folding style is fun to open, but can be challenging to fold back to its original state. Some recipients will not remember how it folded in the first place, and some will lose patience trying to tuck in the final panel. A heavier sheet is recommended.

MODIFICATION
For a softer look, turn the Box Top into a Petal Fold by changing the squared panels into half-circles. The piece is folded the same way and can still serve as a carrier, but the effect is soft and flower-like and is wonderful for special events and invitations.

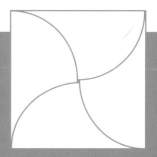

DIGITAL DOCUMENT SIDE 1

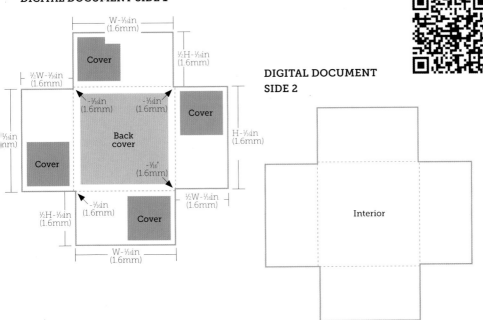

W-¹⁄₁₆in (1.6mm)

½H-¹⁄₁₆in (1.6mm)

½W-¹⁄₁₆in (1.6mm)

-¹⁄₁₆in (1.6mm)   -¹⁄₁₆in (1.6mm)

Cover

Back cover

Cover

Cover

H-¹⁄₁₆in (1.6mm)

-¹⁄₁₆" (1.6mm)

-¹⁄₁₆in (1.6mm)

½H-¹⁄₁₆in (1.6mm)

Cover

½W-¹⁄₁₆in (1.6mm)

W-¹⁄₁₆in (1.6mm)

DIGITAL DOCUMENT SIDE 2

Interior

H = Finished height
W = Finished width

Panel reduction measurements are suggestions and may vary slightly based on the paper weight or the preference of a print vendor.

HOW TO FOLD

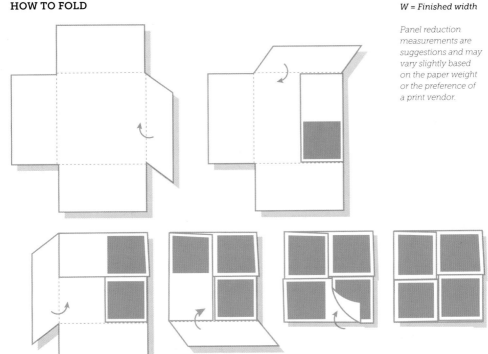

CHECKBOOK FOLD

There are a few variations of the Checkbook Fold, however the general characteristic of this fold is that it opens up and then folds up and out in opposing directions (up and down, or left and right).

This folding style requires a custom die, so work closely with your printer to ensure success. To make the process run even smoother, you may want to ask your printer to provide the die line for you to drop into your digital document.

The Checkbook is a Specialty Fold and for best results should be printed on a heavier sheet. A light sheet will cause the piece to lack structure, and also could make it prone to tearing, since the folding sequence is not always intuitive to the recipient.

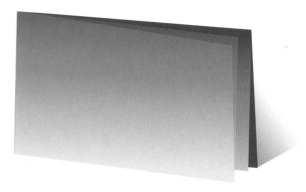

Use for:
Direct mail
Marketing materials
Special events

- -

The Checkbook Fold is not something you see every day. Checkbook Folds are cousins of the Iron Cross Fold, and the beauty of this kind of fold is the seemingly infinite creative possibilities with regard to format, panel count, and shape.

DESIGNERS TIP
This fold requires a custom die, scoring, a heavier sheet, and in most cases, hand-folding. Talk to your printer at the concept stage of the job to make sure your budget can allow for these requirements before selling the idea to your client.

Remember that if you're creating a custom die, nothing says you have to stick to the standard rectangular format. Add a curve or follow the shape of a photo on one of the fold-in panels, or shorten one for a unique reveal. Add a panel or two so that it rolls into itself. Have fun with it!

DIGITAL DOCUMENT SIDE 1

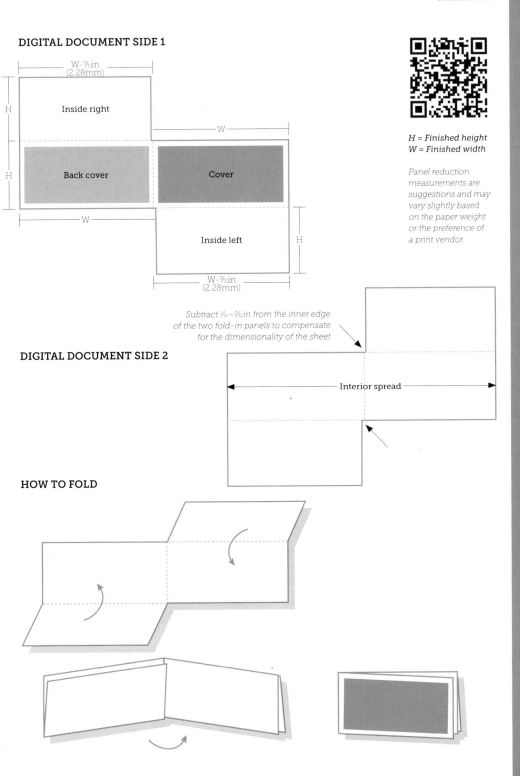

W-³⁄₃₂in
(2.28mm)

H

Inside right

W

H

Back cover

Cover

W

Inside left

H

W-³⁄₃₂in
(2.28mm)

H = Finished height
W = Finished width

Panel reduction measurements are suggestions and may vary slightly based on the paper weight or the preference of a print vendor.

Subtract ¹⁄₁₆ – ³⁄₃₂in from the inner edge of the two fold-in panels to compensate for the dimensionality of the sheet

DIGITAL DOCUMENT SIDE 2

Interior spread

HOW TO FOLD

REVEAL FOLDER

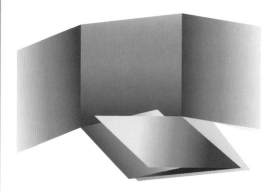

This style offers lots of opportunity for direct mail. In a rectangular format, the piece can meet proper aspect ratio for machinable mailing rates, and the fold-out panels can take the form of coupons or business reply cards (BRCs). Much can be done creatively to captivate the viewer's attention. Since the die is custom-made for this type of specialty fold, consider changing the shape of the panels, or layering die-cuts on each panel to build on a dimensional scene or pattern.

The Reveal Folder is flexible in format and does not have to finish as a square. Square-format mail forces a significant jump in postage costs, due to non-machinability. The Reveal Folder requires scoring, die-cutting, and can be folded by hand or by machine.

Suggested uses:
Direct mail
Promotion
Special events
Specialty/novelty projects

- -

The Reveal Folder is a relative of the Iron Cross Fold whose panels fold out to the left and right, and then a center panel folds downward (or upward) to reveal two more panels that fold out to the sides.

MODIFICATION
Crank up the intensity and turn the six-panel Reveal Folder into a nine-panel Reveal Folder by adding another set of panels to fold up or down and out from the top or bottom edge of the cover. This increases the level of difficulty of the die, as well as the amount of handwork, but for the right project the result can be very exciting.

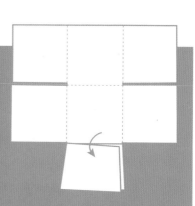

DIGITAL DOCUMENT SIDE 1

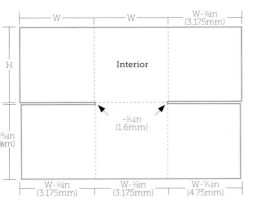

├─ W ─┤─ W ─┤ W-⅛in
(3.175mm)

H

Interior

-1⁄16in
(1.6mm)

⅛in
(m)

W-⅛in
(3.175mm)   W-⅛in
(3.175mm)   W-³⁄16in
(4.75mm)

DIGITAL DOCUMENT SIDE 2

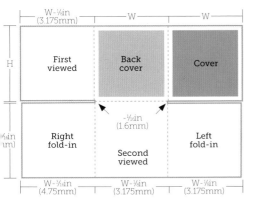

W-⅛in
(3.175mm)   W   W

H

First
viewed

Back
cover

Cover

-1⁄16in
(1.6mm)

⅛in
(m)

Right
fold-in

Left
fold-in

Second
viewed

W-³⁄16in
(4.75mm)   W-⅛in
(3.175mm)   W-⅛in
(3.175mm)

H = Finished height
W = Finished width

*Panel reduction
measurements are
suggestions and may
vary slightly based
on the paper weight
or the preference of
a print vendor.*

HOW TO FOLD

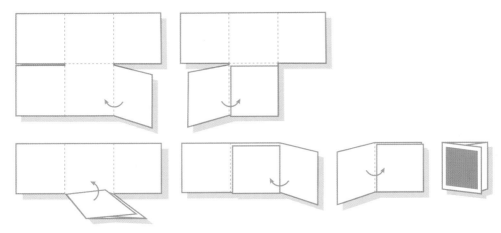

ANGLED ROLL FOLD

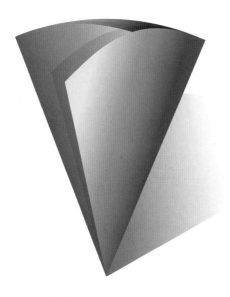

Triangular folds can be great fun. However, they can also be gimmicky, so be sure to choose the right project. Odd shapes are harder to store, carry, and can show wear and tear faster than square or rectangular materials. For example, the pointed tip of a triangle-shaped piece can get crunched into something that looks like a witch's hat if you are not careful—but with the right paper choice and delivery method, this folding style is a real show-off.

To mail this piece, it must be enclosed in an envelope—and for best results through the mail, it may arrive in better condition if the envelope also contains a rectangular postcard or folded piece for additional stability. The Angled Roll Fold requires scoring, die-cutting, and hand-folding.

Suggested uses:
Direct mail
Promotion
Special events
Specialty/novelty projects

- -

The Angled Roll Fold carries the characteristic roll-in panel format of a Roll Fold, with the exception that the folds are at 45° angles to each other. The result is a triangle-shaped piece, and a fun, half-circle shape when laid out flat.

DESIGNER'S TIP
Play with the shape! The half-circle is the standard shape, but this piece requires a custom die and hand-folding anyway, so consider what can be done with angled roll folding, and the flat and finished shapes it can take on. You may be surprised at the possibilities.

DIGITAL DOCUMENT SIDE 1

DIGITAL DOCUMENT SIDE 2

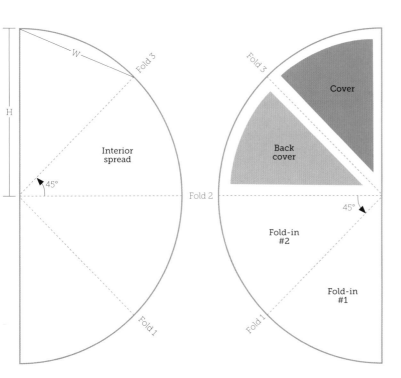

H = Finished height
W = Finished width

This fold can be oriented to present in several directions, for example, party hat (pointing up) or pizza slice (pointing down).

HOW TO FOLD

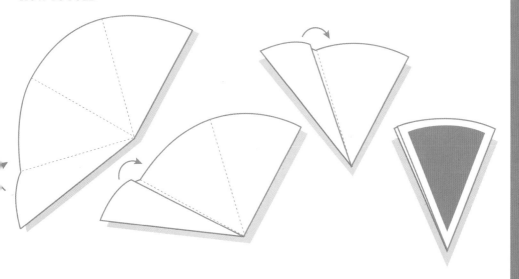

ROLL FOLD WITH NESTED PIECE

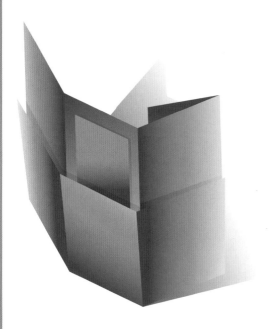

Suggested uses:
Marketing collateral
Promotion
Maps/guides
Brochures
Carrier

- -

The Roll Fold with Nested Piece is a combination fold and a great alternative for the designer who may be considering a pocket folder.

This style begins by adding an inverted short fold to a four-panel Roll Fold. This means that a short fold is folded up from the bottom (rather than down from the top) of the piece. The short fold is folded to the exterior (or cover) side of the piece, and comes up to about half the finished height of the Roll Fold. Once the short fold is in place, the piece is roll folded down to finished size. The tension in the paper creates a tight exterior pocket on the back cover panel.

The final step is to hand-insert a folded piece into the exterior pocket. The folding configuration of the nested piece is not critical. The end result is a stylish glueless pocket solution that can work with or without the insert.

The reason this is considered a folding splurge is not the folding style itself; both styles can be folded by machine. This is a splurge because it requires the creation of two separate folded pieces, and the hand-insertion of the nesting piece into the carrier.

DESIGNER'S TIP
This concept is not just for Roll Folds! For example, add an inverted short fold to the interior of a Tri-Fold and nest a folded piece into the center "pocket." You can also play with the depth of the short fold; try making it higher or lower, add a long diagonal guillotine trim or chop off a corner. If it makes sense conceptually, anything goes.

DIGITAL DOCUMENT SIDE 1

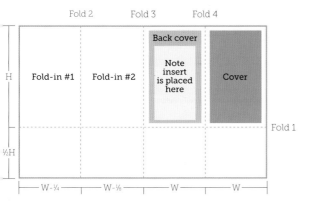

Fold 2   Fold 3   Fold 4

H

½H

Fold-in #1 | Fold-in #2 | Back cover / Note insert is placed here | Cover

Fold 1

W-¼   W-⅛   W   W

H = Finished height
W = Finished width

Insert can be any folding style. However, finished size must be at least ½in (12.7mm) smaller in both height and width than the roll carrier piece.

DIGITAL DOCUMENT SIDE 2

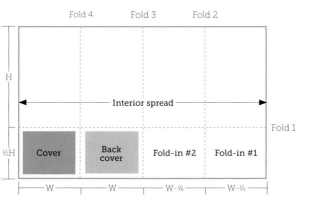

Fold 4   Fold 3   Fold 2

H

½H

Interior spread

Fold 1

Cover | Back cover | Fold-in #2 | Fold-in #1

W   W   W-⅛   W-¼

HOW TO FOLD

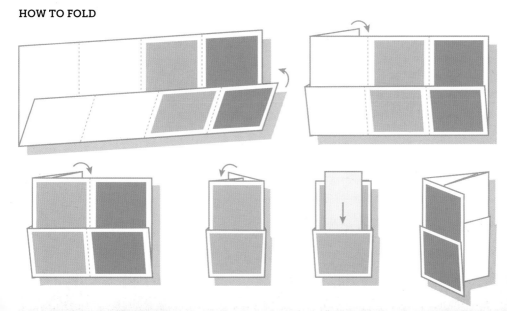

SNAKE FOLD

This particular folding style is rare and exotic, and always makes a statement. The Snake Fold can consist of as few as four panels, and can build up to as many panels as you want, since it is hand-folded; but the longer the Snake Fold, the more unwieldy it can get. This type of novelty fold does not lend itself to text-heavy types of applications. Snake Folds are great for image-heavy projects, invitations, and novelty applications.

Snake Folds do not have to finish as a square format, but this is the most common choice for the style. Square-format mail forces a significant jump in postage costs, due to non-machinability. This fold requires scoring, die-cutting, and hand-folding.

File set-up and paper choice is critical; get your printer involved at an early stage for best results.

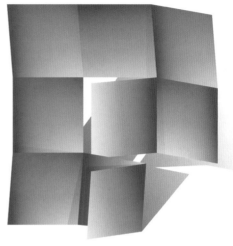

Suggested uses:
Promotion
Special events
Invitations
Specialty/novelty projects

- -

The Snake Fold is a Specialty Fold in which the panels unravel, starting at a center point and working up, over, and around the center like a snake.

DESIGNER'S TIP
Snake Folds are very unusual, and the process of unfolding one is not necessarily intuitive. Make sure the sheet is heavy enough to resist the minor stress inevitable in the unfolding process. The recipient may try to continue to unfold in one direction if they do not realize the direction of the fold just turned 90°, then 90° again, etc. The action could cause unsightly tears in the paper.

DIGITAL DOCUMENT SIDE 1

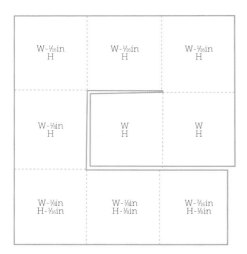

W-⅟₁₆in H	W-⅟₁₆in H	W-⅟₁₆in H
W-⅛in H	W H	W H
W-⅛in H-⅟₁₆in	W-⅛in H-⅛in	W-³⁄₁₆in H-⅛in

H = Finished height
W = Finished width

DIGITAL DOCUMENT SIDE 2

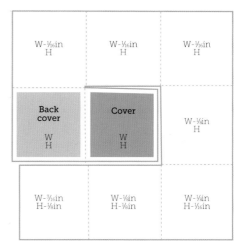

W-⅟₁₆in H	W-⅟₁₆in H	W-⅟₁₆in H
Back cover W H	Cover W H	W-⅛in H
W-³⁄₁₆in H-⅛in	W-⅛in H-⅛in	W-⅛in H-⅟₁₆in

HOW TO FOLD

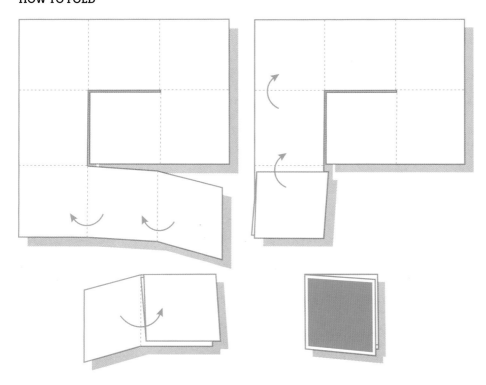

TRAVELING SNAKE FOLD

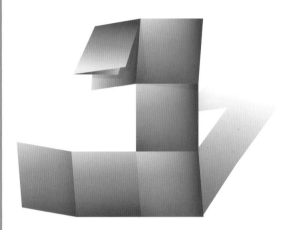

Suggested uses:
Promotion
Special events
Invitations
Specialty/novelty projects

- -

The Traveling Snake Fold features panels that travel around, over, and down in either a random or set pattern. The Traveling Snake is less predictable than a standard Snake Fold, and can be configured in limitless combinations.

Snake Folds are very unusual, and the process of unfolding one is not necessarily intuitive. Make sure the sheet is heavy enough to resist the minor stress that is almost inevitable in the unfolding process. The recipient may try to continue to unfold in one direction if they do not realize the direction of the fold just turned 90°. The action could cause unsightly tears in the paper.

The Traveling Snake does not have to finish as a square format, but this is the most common choice for the style. Square-format mail forces a significant jump in postage costs, due to non-machinability. This fold requires scoring, die-cutting, and hand-folding. File set-up and paper choice is critical; get your printer involved at an early stage for best results.

DESIGNER'S TIP
This type of novelty fold does not lend itself to text-heavy types of applications. Snake Folds are great for image-heavy projects, invitations, and novelty applications. This folding style is fun, and it can be tempting to make it super-long, but be mindful that the longer the Snake Fold, the more unwieldy it will get—which can frustrate rather than captivate the recipient.

DIGITAL DOCUMENT SIDE 1   DIGITAL DOCUMENT SIDE 2

H = Finished height
W = Finished width

Side 1:

W-¼in H-⁵⁄₃₂in	W-⅛in H-⁵⁄₃₂in
W-³⁄₃₂in H-¹⁄₁₆in	W-³⁄₃₂in H-⅛in
W-³⁄₃₂in H	
W-¹⁄₁₆in H	Back cover W H	Cover W H

Side 2:

W-⅛in H-⁵⁄₃₂in	W-⅛in H-⁵⁄₃₂in
	W-³⁄₃₂in H-⅛in	W-³⁄₃₂in H-¹⁄₁₆in
	W-³⁄₃₂in H
W H	W H	W-¹⁄₁₆in H

HOW TO FOLD

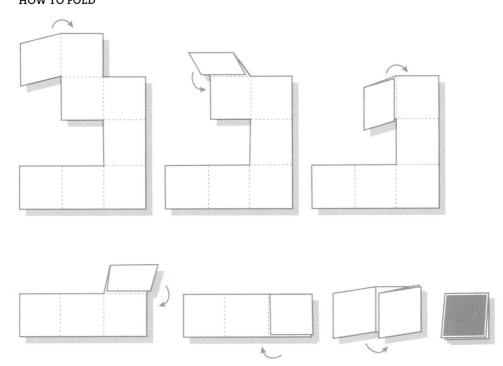

TWIST FOLD

This folding style has a real wow factor and makes for a nice "package." Design square or fancy-shaped inserts to be placed inside. Be sure the dimensions of the insert are at least ⅛in (3.17mm) smaller than the finished dimension of the piece. The inserts will have to be hand-inserted, which will add to the production cost.

The Twist Fold must finish to a square format, and will require an envelope for mailing purposes. Square-format mail forces a significant jump in postage costs, due to non-machinability. This style requires scoring and handwork unless automated at a specialty bindery.

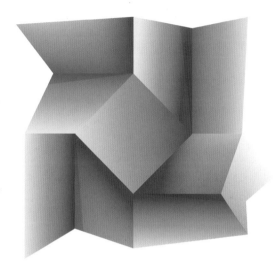

Suggested uses:
Promotion
Special events
Invitations
Specialty/novelty projects
Carrier

- -

The Twist Fold uses a series of perpendicular folds to "twist" a large square sheet down to a compact folded package. The reveal is exceptional. The twisting movement locks the cover closed, so that you do not need a tab.

DESIGNER'S TIP
One of the benefits of the Twist Fold is the ease with which it folds back to its original shape. Some Specialty Folds can be confusing to reconfigure once they have been opened, but the placement of the scores and the symmetry of the design makes the process smooth and effortless. The viewer will tend to open and close this style several times before putting it down.

DIGITAL DOCUMENT SIDE 1

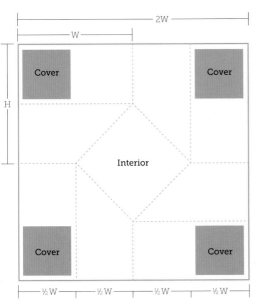

DIGITAL DOCUMENT SIDE 2

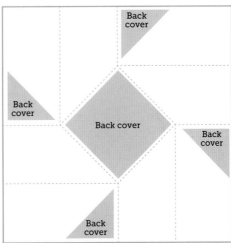

H = Finished height
W = Finished width

HOW TO FOLD

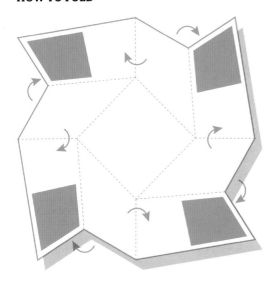

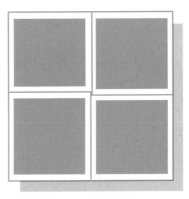

2-WAY CIRCULAR GATE FOLD

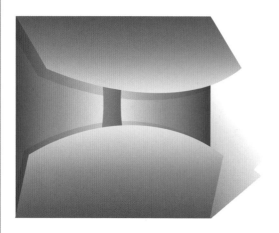

This folding style is one of the more ornamental types of folds, and works extremely well for special events, and for anything with very little content. The fold-in panels do not lend themselves to heavy copy, due to their short, curved shape. Even imagery is a challenge. Trying to crunch a lot of body copy, logos, and photos into the Two-way Circular Gate will look cluttered and amateurish.

This folding style most commonly finishes as a square format, and will require a tab or an envelope for mailing purposes. Square-format mail forces a significant jump in postage costs, due to non-machinability. This style requires die-cutting, scoring, and handwork.

Suggested uses:
Promotion
Special events
Invitations
Specialty/novelty projects
Carrier

- -

The Two-way Circular Gate is a high-impact folding technique that utilizes a circular-shaped die with score. The piece is die-cut into a circle and scored in four places, then hand-folded inward to finish as a square format.

DESIGNER'S TIP
There are many ways to change the mood of a folded piece. This folding style, created with special colored paper and spot inks, can appear formal and luxurious. Choose a white, gloss-coated sheet and you can "dress it down" as a four-color casual invitation to a bowling tournament.

This folding style can hold an insert—be sure the dimensions are at least ⅛in (3.17mm) smaller than the finished dimension of the piece. The inserts will have to be hand-inserted, which will add to the production cost.

DIGITAL DOCUMENT SIDE 1

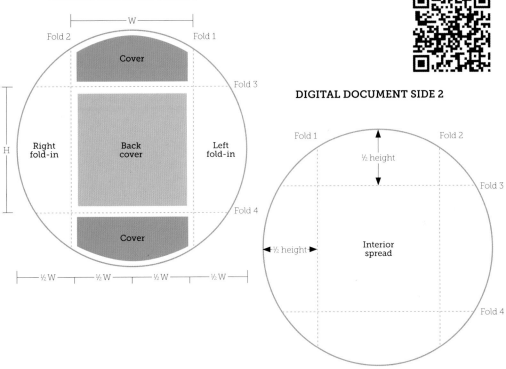

DIGITAL DOCUMENT SIDE 2

H = Finished height
W = Finished width

There is some flexibility with fold placement—folds can be adjusted so panels overlap rather than touch. The diagram illustrates both sets of folding panels meeting in the middle.

HOW TO FOLD

BROADSIDE BOOKLET FOLD

There is a fascinating discovery process due to the multi-page book-like format of the folded piece, followed by the realization that there is something to see underneath it all. This is a great solution for text-heavy content, because of the two-page spreads, and the format is such that the viewer can read the content from start to finish without question of order. In comparison, a fold like the Roll Fold can cause confusion because the viewer may not intuitively follow the designer's intended viewing order.

The Broadside Booklet Fold requires scoring, die-cutting, and in most cases, hand-folding. Paper choice is important because of the right-angle folds needed to create a Broadside Fold—request a few dummies in different weights and finishes to determine the best sheet for your project.

Suggested uses:
Brochures
Promotion
Maps/guides
Direct mail

- -

The Broadside Booklet uses a broadside format with creative placement of a die-cut along the fold of the two center panels. When folded down, the piece takes the form of a booklet, and when unfolded, it takes the form of a poster.

DESIGNER'S TIP
Nobody said you have to use the interior spread for text, imagery, maps, and the like. Cover it with a fabulously rich double hit of spot color, or print an intriguing pattern that peeks out as the viewer flips the page.

DIGITAL DOCUMENT SIDE 1

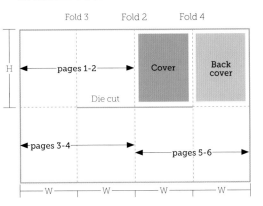

DIGITAL DOCUMENT SIDE 2

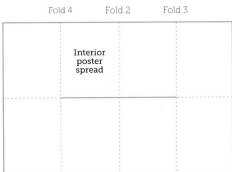

H = Finished height
W = Finished width

HOW TO FOLD

POP-UP FOLD

There are limitless configurations for Pop-ups, and some can be true feats of "paper engineering." In its simplest form, scores or perforations placed at 45° angles to the left and right of a fold force the paper to collapse inward. The angled wedge-shape that results allows for the vertical height of that section to be extended above the top edge of the piece. The taller section tucks down when folded, and pops up when opened.

Additional panels can be added to the folded piece to conceal the unsightly mechanics of the Pop-up. For example, a four-page brochure with a Pop-up in the interior spread will have a clipped upper left corner when the piece is folded. Add two Accordion panels—one extending from the front cover, one extending from the back cover—and the clipped corner disappears.

All Pop-ups are custom designs. This style of fold requires a heavier sheet for structural stability, and hand-folding in most cases. Enlist the close guidance of a printer.

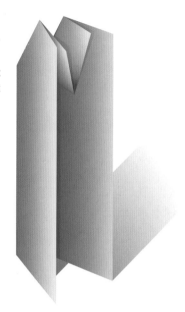

Suggested uses:
Direct mail
Promotion
Greeting cards
Specialty/novelty projects

- -

The Pop-up Fold is a dimensional solution that combines die-cutting, scoring, perforating, and folding. Pop-ups are usually a surprise, hidden in the folded piece, only to be revealed by the motion of opening the piece.

DESIGNER'S TIP
Pop-ups are probably best known in the greeting card aisle, but they can be a fantastic technique for getting attention in the mail. Talk with your printer early on in the creative process to determine the style of Pop-up that suits your project, and to ensure that your die is spot on.

DIGITAL DOCUMENT SIDE 1

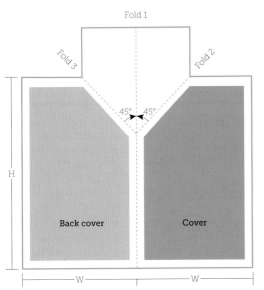

DIGITAL DOCUMENT SIDE 2

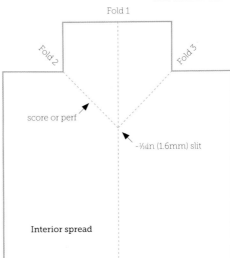

H = Finished height
W = Finished width

The pop-up area can be a variety of shapes, and the angled folds can be wide or narrow. There is a lot of creative flexibility with a pop-up. The diagram depicts the most basic v-format pop-up.

HOW TO FOLD

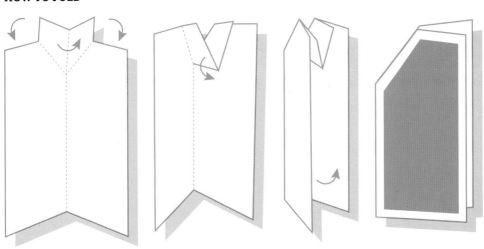

TRIANGLE FOLD

There are many different formats for Triangle Folds. If your paper is light enough and you can fold down to a square format, you can most likely add a final fold on the diagonal. For example, a four-panel Accordion can be folded down to a square and then turned into a Triangle. A Closed Gate Fold or a Tri-Fold can become a Triangle, too. As in most cases with Specialty Folds, the key to success is getting a printer involved at the earliest stages to ensure there are no production issues that would prevent you from producing your design.

Suggested uses:
Direct mail
Promotion
Special events
Specialty/novelty
projects

- -

The Triangle Fold starts as a rectangle and folds down to a triangle using parallel and angled folds. Triangle Folds can be great fun, but they can also seem gimmicky at times, so be sure to choose a project that fits the character of this folding style.

To mail this piece, it must be enclosed in an envelope—and for best results through the mail, it may arrive in better condition if the envelope also contains a rectangular-shaped postcard or folded piece for additional stability. Angled folds are difficult to set up by machine—some printers will fold them by hand and some will automate the process, depending upon quantity.

FACT
Odd shapes are harder to store and carry, and can show wear and tear faster than square or rectangular materials.

DIGITAL DOCUMENT SIDE 1

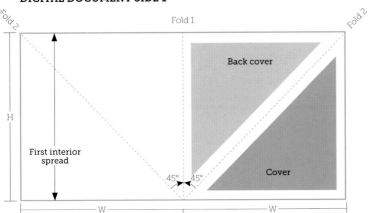

DIGITAL DOCUMENT SIDE 2

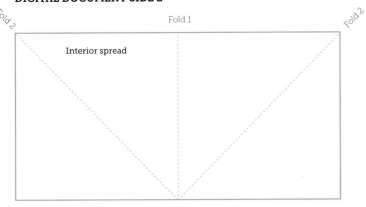

H = Finished height
W = Finished width

HOW TO FOLD

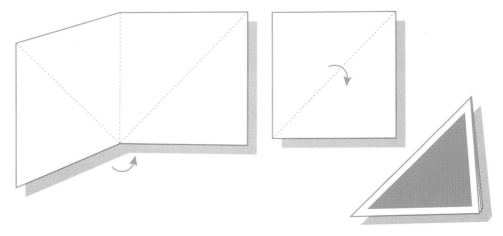

TULIP FOLD

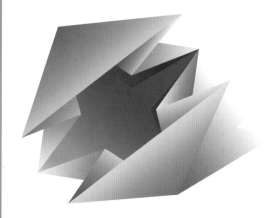

Suggested uses:
Special events
Promotion
Greeting cards
Marketing collateral
Direct mail
Specialty/novelty projects

- -

The Tulip Fold (also known as the Pinch Fold) uses folds on the diagonal to create the effect of a pop-up dimensional piece.

The pure simplicity is beautiful—one of the more artistic of the specialty folding styles, the Tulip Fold can be modified in many ways to create different viewer experiences. The basic principle of this fold is the addition of a fold on the diagonal in selected panels that allow the "pinched" panels to collapse in on themselves and tuck into the panels next to them. When opened, the panels reveal in a flower-like manner (hence the tulip moniker).

Panels can be connected together to create a series of tulip folds, and you can even play with the placement of the diagonal folds to create asymmetrical tulip folded panels. This style of folding is very flexible in that manner.

The Tulip Fold is best produced in a text weight sheet to avoid bulkiness and expansion, and to reduce the likelihood of wrinkles in the corner joints of the folds. Experiment to see which paper weight and finish is best suited to the project.

DESIGNER'S TIP
Even on the right sheet of paper, this folding style can expand a bit, which would make it difficult for auto-insertion into envelopes. One option (for this folding style, or any folding style that may have an expansion issue) would be to consider designing a belly band that slides off before opening.

PRODUCTION TIP
Depending upon the format the designer chooses, this piece can be executed with or without a die-cut. Most printers will choose to score and fold this style by hand; however it is possible to automate certain variations of this folding style.

DIGITAL DOCUMENT SIDE 1

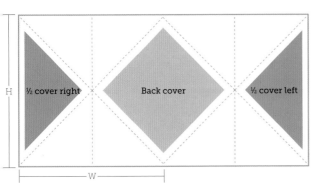

H | ½ cover right   Back cover   ½ cover left

W

H = Finished height
W = Finished width

DIGITAL DOCUMENT SIDE 2

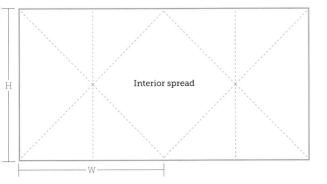

H | Interior spread

W

HOW TO FOLD

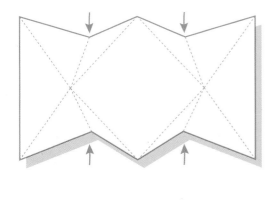

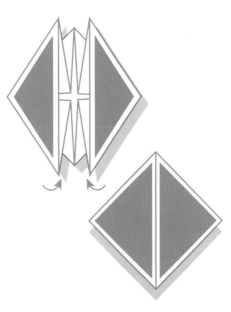

GALLERY

*This Iron Cross Fold with
layered die-cuts on all
four fold-in panels was
a self-promotional piece
for Whitmore Group*

V-format Pop-up mailer for Circus (airdate: 2010 on PBS); © PBS 2011; circus piece: design by Christopher Richard; production by Westland Printers

Square-format direct mail "cube" produced by Schmitz Press

The three-piece product had a cube-shaped top that slid off to reveal a starburst-like interior folded piece and an accordion-folded reply card.

Folded, the dimensionality of this piece is not obvious, however when unfolded, the clever format reveals a self-standing piece. Stepped Accordion/Swinger combo fold by ColorCraft of Virginia (left)

A well-placed die-cut can work with the folds to create dimension. Swinger Fold holiday card from Sametz Blackstone Associates (below)

*Traveling Snake
Fold designed by
Miller Brooks*

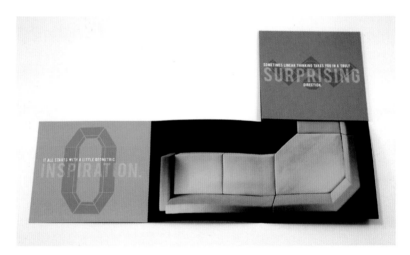

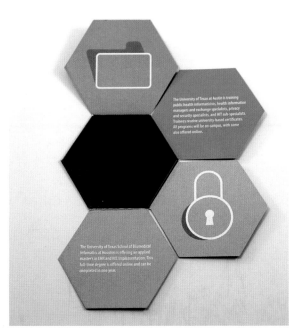

Hexagon-shaped
Iron-cross fold by Julie
Babler, Mary Love
Bigony, Hoyt Haffelder,
and Chandler Prude;
Texas State University

CHAPTER FIVE: RESOURCES

The materials on the following pages are intended to serve as useful resources when you're in the planning stages of a folded print project.

• In this section you'll learn a lot about setting up a digital document for folded material. There's a lot to think about, and proper technique can mean the difference between expensive alterations by the printer, and a file that sails through prepress.

• There is important information about how mechanical folding is carried out. It is always good to understand the process. Once you understand how it works, and how you can push the medium creatively, you might find it helpful to see the process in action. Call your local printer or bindery and ask for a tour.

• You'll find envelope styles and sizes, common sheet sizes, links to more folding resources, and a glossary.

• You will also find information about using the files provided on the CD, and helpful tips for how to create your own production file if you find you need to modify a fold from this book, or if you're feeling adventurous and want to create something entirely new.

More than meets the eye
In this section we're listing *common* sizes for paper and envelopes, but there are always exceptions. So, if you're looking for (or have heard of) a size and you don't see it listed, don't worry— just do your homework. There are other less common sheet sizes and of course custom and special order envelope sizes as well. You just may have to look a little harder for them.

TIPS FOR PROPER SET-UP OF FOLDED MATERIALS

USING THE TEMPLATES PROVIDED ON THE CD

The templates are provided in two file formats—Adobe Illustrator EPS files, and Adobe Acrobat PDF files. The files are named by the associated page number and then by side, A or B. Side A is the front, side B is the back. If a template is labeled AB, it is because the back and front fold placement is identical, and therefore the AB file may be used for both sides of the folded piece.

The EPS files include the die-line only, however the PDF files include a bleed zone and crop marks for guidance. Bleeds should always extend at least ⅛in (3.17mm) past the edge of the die-line.

Each template was created in one finished size, however that template can be scaled up or down to change the size proportionately by holding the Shift key and dragging while the object is selected. To convert the templates to a custom size, it is recommended that the mathematics provided in the diagram on the coordinating page in the book are followed instead. You may be able to adjust the provided template, but in some cases, it may be easier to create the die-line from scratch.

Page layout can be executed in Adobe Illustrator if desired, however, it is recommended that the EPS of the die-line or the PDF is imported into a professional page layout software containing two pages—one for side A and one for side B.

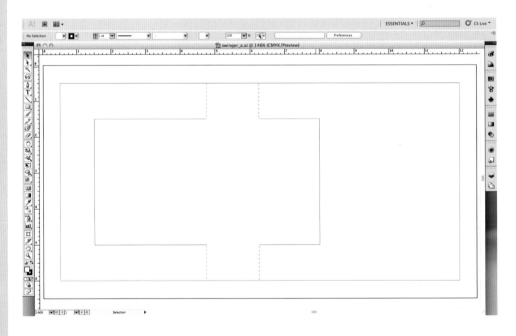

An Adobe Illustrator template

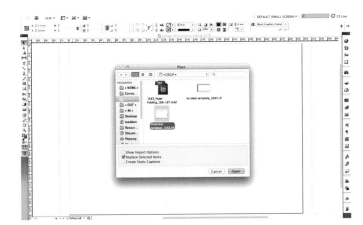

*Placing an Illustrator template
into an InDesign document.*

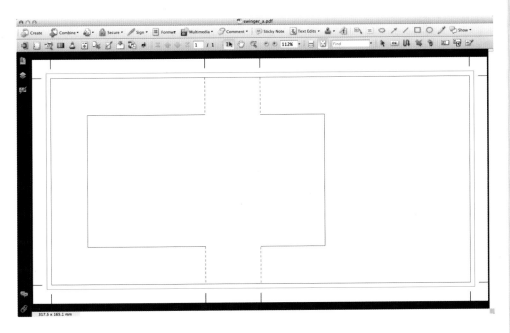

A PDF template displayed in Adobe Acrobat

CREATING A CUSTOM DIE-LINE

Don't be intimidated if you need to create your own custom die-line for a folded project. The technique is easy. The main principal to keep in mind is accuracy. The printer will make their die from the line work you provide, so there is no room for error. If you cannot guarantee accuracy, you may want to ask your printer for help creating the die-line instead.

To begin, launch an illustration or page layout software that is capable of creating vector line art, such as Adobe Illustrator, Adobe InDesign, or QuarkXPress. Next, create a layer and name it "Die-line Layer." This layer will hold *only* the art created for the die-line. Creating a separate layer for the die-line allows the printer to isolate the art and either print it or suppress the printout of the art on the layer.

Grab your pen or straight line tool, adjust the stroke width to 0.5pt and set the color to a spot color (see Inset 1), and use that spot color for the die-line *only*. Again, this allows the printer to isolate and print the die-line as a separate "color." This is an important detail. Once you've created the layer and set the stroke, you can draw the desired shape. Areas that will be cut must utilize solid strokes, and to indicate the exact placement of folds, the stroke must be dashed (see Inset 2).

Construction of the die-line will likely require generous usage of guides and rulers to assure accuracy. Once the die-line is complete, print it out, trim it down, and fold it to be sure your work is perfect.

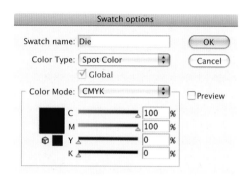

Inset 1

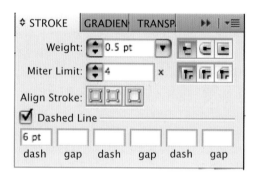

Inset 2

PLACING FOLD MARKS IN A DOCUMENT

A die-line is only necessary for materials that require a custom cutting process. Many of the uniquely-shaped folding styles in the Folding Splurges chapter of this book require a die, however, folded materials that do not require a die also require the proper technique to ensure success.

The first thing to do is to calculate document size. The document should be built to trim size, so looking at the diagram provided in the book, calculate the appropriate reductions in both height and width to get a finished trim size. That number will become the page size of your digital document.

Launching your page layout software, enter the finished dimension and make sure rulers and guides are visible. Create a two-page document (unless the project will only be printed on one side). Depending upon the orientation of the folds, measure the first panel to the measurement indicated on the diagram, and release a vertical or horizontal guide.

After you've placed the first guide, it may be easier to drag the crosshairs from the upper left corner of the ruler and release at the guide you just set. This allows you to measure a panel from zero again, rather than counting up from the first panel width. You can do this each time you set a guide if you prefer this technique.

DESIGNER TIP

Always build an accurate file first. It's tempting to dive right into layout with sloppy file set-up and the best of intentions to deal with the technical stuff later. We all know that time gets tight at the end, and there's never enough time to focus on the details when you're up against the clock. Creating a proper file at the end may also shift margins, crops on photos, and line breaks, and may add an annoying and unnecessary additional round of approvals from the client.

Continue to drop guides in the suggested positions until all folds are indicated with a guide. For page two of your digital document, pay close attention to the diagram, as oftentimes the folds are in different positions on the opposing side.

Once the guides have been set, it's time to place the fold marks. To do this is simple. Draw a short, dashed line directly above the first guide and aligning with that guide exactly, making sure that it's only in the slug area and not on the printable area (see Marks 1). Then, follow the guide straight down and make another short dashed line just below the guide, aligning with the guide. Zoom out and group the two dashed lines, copy and paste the grouped lines, and place them at the next guide. Repeat until all of the guides have fold marks (see Marks 2).

When you've set them all for both pages, print the document (be sure to check the print preference to "include slug area"), trim it out, fold it down, and make sure you didn't misplace or miscalculate the fold placements. If there are no problems, you're ready to start your layout.

GENERAL GUIDELINES FOR CREATING FOLDED MATERIALS

- The general rule for one single sheet thickness folding into another is to shorten the fold-in panel by $3/32$–$1/8$in (2.28–3.17mm).

- If the fold-in panel is broadside (double sheet thickness) or in heavy cover stock, subtract $1/8$–$3/16$in (3.17–4.76mm) from the panel width to compensate for pushout from the underlying piece of paper or the weight of the cover stock.

- The more layers of paper, the lighter the sheet should be, and the greater the folding compensation amount. Work closely with a printer or paper representative to make sure your paper choice is appropriate for the folding solution.

- This book will inspire lots of new folding ideas that may be new iterations of the designs featured on these pages. If you come up with something new, be sure to consult with your printer or bindery first before selling the concept to a client. What may seem like a small tweak to you could possibly turn a low-budget option into a high-budget specialty fold.

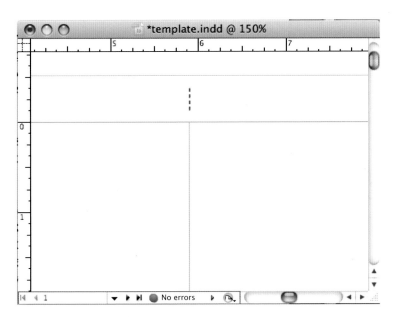

Marks 1

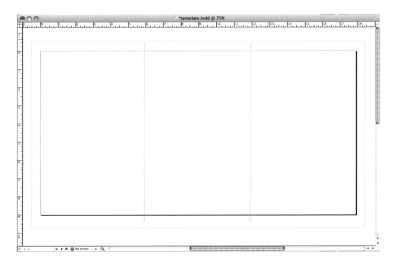

Marks 2

MECHANICAL FOLDING TECHNIQUES

Folding by hand is a necessity for mock-ups and specialty folds, but when folding for mass production, finishing by machine is the fastest, most efficient way to get the job done. In the process of mechanical folding, there are three commonly used techniques—knife folding, buckle folding, and plow folding. One mechanical folding process may suit a specific project, while another may require a combination of techniques.

KNIFE FOLDING

Knife folding uses a vertically-moving knife and two rollers rotating in opposite directions (see illustration below). The sheet is carried from the feed to the folding station until it makes contact with the sheet stop. At this point, the knife descends vertically, plunging the sheet between the rollers that have been set to the thickness of the sheet going through them. As the sheet passes through the rollers, it is pinched and the fold is formed. This folding process depends upon the repetitive action of the knife.

Only one folding knife is to be found in any one folding station. For every subsequent fold, it is necessary to have a further knife folding station at right angles to the preceding one. Printers and binders specializing in folding large sheets usually use knife folders.

BUCKLE FOLDING

A buckle-folding station consists of three rollers and a buckle plate (see illustration at right). The first two rollers are arranged

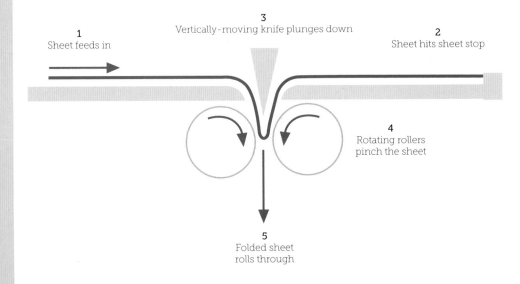

1
Sheet feeds in

3
Vertically-moving knife plunges down

2
Sheet hits sheet stop

4
Rotating rollers
pinch the sheet

5
Folded sheet
rolls through

vertically above one another and their job is to carry the incoming sheet into the buckle plate until it reaches an adjustable feed guide stop.

The sheet is delivered into the buckle plate at a speed determined by the characteristics of the paper. As the lead edge of the sheet strikes the feed guide stop, the sheet continues to be fed into the buckle plate, creating a buckle in the space between the three rollers. As the excess paper drives downward, it is grabbed by the contra-rotating rollers and the fold is formed as the sheet passes through them.

Unlike knife folding, buckle folding is not restricted to any cyclical movement, making it ideal for high-speed folding. Most folding stations can fit up to six buckle plates, arranged alternately above and below each other, allowing for a large number of fold variations.

PLOW FOLDING

Plow folding uses a stationary metal plow with the edges inclined at an angle to the flow direction of the paper. As the sheet travels over the plow, it folds over parallel to the flow direction. Plow folders employ a fold "former" made of shaped sheet metal or folding rods that guide the sheet as it goes over the stationary plow, allowing for a clean edge on the fold.

Plow folding is commonly used to convert packaging, because board weight stocks cannot be buckle or knife folded. It is also employed for inline web finishing, with tension in the web so that the paper tracks over the fold plows consistently. Plow folding is not as common for folding brochures and lighter weight stocks that could easily be folded with a buckle folder, however, with the appropriate equipment it can be done.

Folding Fact
Virtually any folding style—no matter how complicated—can be folded by a machine if the quantity is high enough. It has to be worth the time, effort, and expense to set up the machinery to do it. That's why many tricky (and some not so tricky) folds are finished by hand.

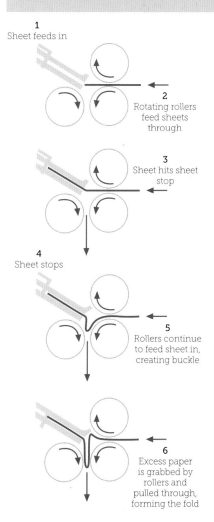

1
Sheet feeds in

2
Rotating rollers feed sheets through

3
Sheet hits sheet stop

4
Sheet stops

5
Rollers continue to feed sheet in, creating buckle

6
Excess paper is grabbed by rollers and pulled through, forming the fold

SHEET SIZES

Below is a list of the most common sheet sizes for offset, web, and digital printing. Not all sizes are inventoried by all paper companies and distributors, and may not be available in text and cover weights. Plan ahead. Ask your printer or paper representative about available weights and sheet sizes before settling on a particular paper. Remember that you are limited to the maximum press sheet size that your printer's equipment can handle.

COMMON US SHEET SIZES: OFFSET PRINTING

US (in)	Metric (mm)
17½ x 22½	444.5 x 571.5
19 x 25	482.6 x 635
20 x 26	508 x 660.4
23 x 29	584.2 x 736.6
23 x 35	584.2 x 889
24 x 36	609.6 x 914.4
25 x 38	635 x 965.2
26 x 40	660.4 x 1,016
28 x 40	711.2 x 1,016
35 x 45	889 x 1,143
38 x 50	965.2 x 1,270

COMMON US ROLL WIDTHS: WEB OFFSET PRINTING

US (in)	Metric (mm)
17½	444.5
18	457.2
23	548.2
23½	596.9
26½	673.1
33	838.2
33½	850.9
34½	876.3
35	889
35½	901.7
38	965.2

COMMON US SHEET SIZES: DIGITAL PRINTING

US (in)	Metric (mm)
11 x 17	279.4 x 431.8
12 x 18	304.8 x 457.2
13 x 19	330.2 x 482.6
14 x 20	355.6 x 508
14⅓ x 20½	363.22 x 520.7

COMMON US ROLL WIDTHS: DIGITAL WEB PRINTING

US (in)	Metric (mm)
13	330.2
15	381
18	457.2
18½	469.9
19	482.6
19½	495.3
20	508

EUROPEAN/ISO SHEET SIZES (mm)

Sheet size	A	B	C	RA	SRA
0	841 x 1,189	1,000 x 1,414	917 x 1,296	860 x 1,220	900 x 1,280
1	594 x 841	707 x 1,000	648 x 917	610 x 860	640 x 900
2	420 x 594	500 x 707	458 x 648	430 x 610	450 x 640
3	297 x 420	353 x 500	324 x 458	305 x 430	320 x 450
4	210 x 297	250 x 353	229 x 324	215 x 305	225 x 320
5	148 x 210	176 x 250	162 x 229	152 x 215	160 x 225
6	105 x 148	125 x 176	114 x 162	107 x 152	112 x 160
7	74 x 105	88 x 125	81 x 114	76 x 107	80 x 112
8	52 x 74	62 x 88	57 x 81	53 x 76	56 x 80

STANDARD ENVELOPE SIZES

EUROPEAN SIZES

Number	Height (mm)	Width (mm)	Height (in)	Width (in)
C7	81	114	3.19	4.49
C7/6	81	162	3.19	6.38
DL	110	220	4.33	8.66
C6	114	162	4.49	6.38
B6	125	176	4.92	6.93
½ BC4	125	324	4.92	12.75
E6	140	200	5.51	7.87
C5	162	229	6.38	9.02
B5	176	250	6.93	9.84
E5	200	280	7.87	11.02
C4	229	324	9.02	12.75
B4	250	353	9.84	13.09
E4	280	400	11.02	15.75

These sizes are used in all European countries, except Great Britain. In Great Britain, A4 (210 x 297 mm / 4.25 x 8.625 inches) is the standard size for a folded letterhead. The dimensions of an A4 envelope are 324 x 229 mm / 12.75 x 9 inches.

COMMON ENVELOPE STYLES

A-style with square flap   Catalog   Baronial

AMERICAN SIZES:
Announcement and Commercial

Number	Size (mm)	Size (in)
A-2	111 x 146	4⅜ x 5¾
A-6	120 x 165	4¾ x 6½
A-7	139 x 184	5¼ x 7¼
A-8	139 x 206	5½ x 8⅛
A-10	159 x 244	6¼ x 9⅝
Slim	98 x 225	3⅞ x 8⅞
No. 6¼	89 x 152	3½ x 6
No. 6¾	92 x 165	3⅝ x 6½
No. 8	98 x 190	3⅞ x 7½
No. 9	98 x 225	3⅞ x 8⅞
No. 10	105 x 241	4⅛ x 9½
No. 11	114 x 263	4½ x 10⅜
No. 12	120 x 279	4¾ x 11
No.14	127 x 292	5 x 11½

AMERICAN SIZES:
Catalog

Number	Size (mm)	Size (in)
No. 1	152 x 228	6 x 9
No.1¾	165 x 241	6½ x 9½
No. 2	165 x 254	6½ x 10
No. 3	178 x 254	7 x 10
No. 6	190 x 266	7½ x 10½
No. 7	203 x 279	8 x 11
No. 8	209 x 286	8¼ x 11¼
No. 9½	216 x 267	8½ x 10½
No. 9¾	222 x 286	8¾ x 11¼
No. 10½	229 x 305	9 x 12
No. 12½	241 x 317	9½ x 12½
No. 13½	254 x 330	10 x 13
No. 14¼	286 x 311	11¼ x 12¼
No. 14½	292 x 368	11½ x 14½

Commercial

Booklet

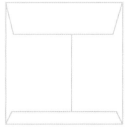

Square

USEFUL WEBSITES

foldfactory
Professionals go to foldfactory for
production-perfect folding templates,
folding tips, tools, resources, and endless
inspiration. Search the industry's only 3D
folding sample library for Accordion Folds,
Gate Folds, Roll Folds, specialty and
proprietary folding, and much more. Join
foldfactory's free educational community
and start receiving the "60-second Super-
cool Fold of the Week."
www.foldfactory.com

Between the Folds
Documentary film about the science, art, and
ingenuity of the world's best paper folders.
www.greenfusefilms.com

The Fold Picker
This two-sided publication offers 30 low-to-
moderate budget "frugal" folding ideas in one
direction, and with a simple flip, offers 30
high-budget "fabulous" folding splurges in the
other direction. All of the folding styles featured
in the Picker have coordinating videos posted
on foldfactory.com. Produced by foldfactory.
com and Sappi Fine Paper.
www.mydesignshop.com/product/
fold-picker

The Paper Mill Store
The Paper Mill Store offers the widest selection
of specialty paper cardstock, and envelopes for
paper enthusiasts and graphics professionals
in reams, boxes, or in bulk, from top paper
mills, shipped from their Paper Valley
Wisconsin warehouse.
papermillstore.com

Paper Resources
Paper advisers who can meet all the needs
of those sourcing fine papers from around
the world.
www.paperresources.co.uk

PaperSpecs
The first online paper database specifically
developed for the design and print industri
The PaperSpecs database features more tha
4,300 papers—from opaque to recycled, fro
translucent to digital—helping you to find
perfect paper for your vision within minute
PaperSpecs doesn't sell paper, they simply
you everything you need to know about it.
tips, webinars, and more!
www.paperspecs.com

Popular Kinetics Press
This site offers amazing books, tutorials, ar
information about making pop-ups and
dimensional publications.
popularkinetics.com

The Standard 4: Scoring & Folding
Not just a high-quality paper manufacture
Sappi also has a long history of producing
beautiful, informative, and free educationa
materials for the graphic arts industry. Che
out their series called "The Standard." Volur
features Scoring and Folding—it's beautifu
produced and packed with ideas.
sappi.com/na

Upon a Fold
Australia-based online shop and blog run k
graphic designers with a passion for paper
The blog showcases inspiring paper artistr
from around the world, from jewelry and
fashion to pop-ups and stationery.
www.uponafold.com.au

CONTRIBUTORS

3D Paper Graphics
www.3dpapergraphics.com

Acculink
www.acculink.com

Americhip
www.americhip.com

Barbara Cooper Design
barbaracooperdesign.com

B.Moss
www.b-moss.com

Chartreuse
chartreuseinc.com

ColorCraft of Virginia
www.colorcraft-va.com

Compass Maps Ltd.
www.popoutproducts.com

Davidson Belluso
www.davidsonbelluso.com

Design Ranch
www.design-ranch.com

GV Creative
gvcreative.com

Impressive Print
Impressiveprint.com

Isabel Uria
isabeluria.com

ITP
www.itpofusa.com

J Kozak Creative
www.jkozakcreative.com

Kanella Arapoglou
www.kanella.com

Kelsey Grafton
www.kelseygrafton.com

Keystone Resources
www.keystone-resources.com

Maureen Weiss Design
maureenweiss.com

Miller Brooks
www.millerbrooks.com

Molly McCoy
www.mollymccoy.com

Neenah Paper
www.neenahpaper.com

Oliver Printing Co.
www.oliverprinting.com

PBS
pbs.org

Phillips Graphic Finishing
www.phillipsgraphicfinishing.com

Premier Press
www.premierpress.com

Publicis New York
Philip Arias, Jeremy Filgate
www.publicis-usa.com

Sametz Blackstone Associates
www.sametz.com

Sandstrom Partners
www.sandstrompartners.com

Sappi Fine Paper
www.sappi.com/na

Schmitz Press
schmitzpress.com

Smithsonian National Museum of Natural History
www.mnh.si.edu

Specialties Graphic Finishers
www.specialtiesgraphics.com

Standard
www.sdmc.com

Structural Graphics
www.structuralgraphics.com

Suttle Straus
www.suttle-straus.com

Technifold USA
www.technifoldusa.com

Texas State University: Julie Babler, Mary Love Bigony, Hoyt Haffelder, Chandler Prude
www.txstate.edu

Upshift Creative Group
upshiftcreative.com

UVIAUS
uviaus.com

Whitmore Group
www.whitmore.com

Westland Printers
www.westlandprinters.com

Z-CARD North America
www.zcardna.com

GLOSSARY

Accordion fold
Two or more parallel folds that go in opposite directions, forming a "zig-zag" appearance.

Against the grain
Perpendicular (at a 90° angle) to the direction of the grain in the paper.

Bind
To join pages of a book together with materials such as thread, adhesive, wire, coarse fabric (crash), etc. The bound pages are commonly enclosed in a cover.

Bindery
A facility where post-press finishing operations are performed, such as folding, binding, foil stamping, inserting, and more.

Bleed
Ink coverage that extends past the edge of the trim edge to compensate for movement on press and trim variations in the finishing stages. A designer should "pull bleeds" at least ⅛in (3.17mm) past the document edge before sending a digital file to the printer.

Broadside fold
A broadside-style fold doubles its area by folding in half on itself before any characteristic folding style is created. For example, a broadside letter fold is 12 pages, whereas the standard letter fold is six.

Bulk
The thickness of a single sheet of paper, expressed in points. A point is ¹⁄₁₀₀₀ of an inch.

Caliper
The measure of paper thickness expressed in thousandths of an inch.

Converting
The processing of paper to produce another paper product, such as envelopes, cartons, brochures, or folders.

Cover paper
Heavy-weight, coated, or uncoated paper with a basis size of 20 x 26in (508 x 660.4mm) most often used for covers, folders, greeting and business cards, and other applications that require a heavier sheet.

Cracking
The breaking of paper fibers at the fold caused by the stress of the folding process. Cracking is most noticeable when the fold is covered with ink, or when the sheet is very heavy. Scoring is the easiest way to prevent cracking at the fold.

Cross-grain
Folding at a right angle to the direction of the grain in the paper stock. Also known as "against the grain."

Cutter
A machine for cutting paper stock, also known as a guillotine cutter.

Die
A pattern of sharp knives or metal tools used to crease, stamp, cut, perforate, or emboss into a substrate.

Die-cut
Using sharp steel rules to cut paper or board into a specified shape.

Die-line
For the die-making process, a line drawn by the designer or prepress professional that shows the print-finisher where to place the die.

Dog-ear
An unsightly bend at the corner of a folded sheet, caused by snagging in the folding machinery or poor handling.

Finished size
The final measurements of a printed piece after converting (folding, trimming, etc.).

Finished length
The final length measurement of a printed piece after converting (folding, trimming, etc.).

Finished width
The final width measurement of a printed piece after converting (folding, trimming, etc.).

Finishing
Also called post-press, finishing is any operation completed after the printing process. This includes, binding, folding, saddlestitching, bundling, coating, cutting, die-cutting, drilling, embossing, glue and wafer seals, collating, tipping-on, inserting, and more. Finishing units may be offline or attached to the end of the press.

Flat size
The exact dimensions of a finished printed piece when laid out flat.

Fold
Bending and creasing a sheet of paper to virtually eliminate the paper's natural tendency to revert to its original shape.

Fold indication mark
Visual guide that indicates where a printed piece will fold. Normally shown as a dotted line.

Folder
Machinery that automates the creasing of printed sheets of paper to particular specifications.

Folding dummy
A mock-up that shows the print-finisher exactly how the printed piece is intended to fold.

Gate fold
When two or more panels fold in toward the center from opposing sides.

Grain direction
In commercial papermaking, the alignment of fibers in the direction of web travel.

Grain direction, against
Folding or cutting paper at right angles to the paper grain.

Grain direction, with
Folding or cutting paper parallel to the paper grain.

Inline finishing
Manufacturing operations such as numbering, addressing, sorting, folding, scoring, die-cutting, and converting that are performed as part of a continuous operation that occurs on press right after the printing process or on a single piece of equipment as part of the folding/binding process.

Kiss-cut
For peel-off labels, to die-cut the top layer but not the backing of self-adhesive paper.

Offline finishing
Altering printed materials to form the final printed piece or product on a machine separate from the printing press. Printers may have their own finishing equipment or they may send the work to companies that specialize in finishing.

Page
One side of a panel.

Panel
A two-sided segment of a folded piece, defined by the crease of a fold or the trimmed edge.

Parallel fold
Folds made in parallel to each other.

Perforation
Punching a row of small holes or incisions into a sheet of paper to make it easier to detach, to allow air to escape from signatures, or to help prevent wrinkling when folded.

Pop-up
A sheet that is specially cut and folded so that, when opened, it takes on a 3-D effect.

Post-press
See Finishing.

Proprietary folds
These are formats and structures owned and patented as Intellectual Property by individuals or companies. Permission must be obtained for their use. Third-party usage rights are sometimes granted under a royalty or licensing agreement, but at the sole discretion of the patent holder.

Right-angle fold
A fold that is perpendicular to another fold.

Roll fold
When paper is folded two or more times in the same direction, creating a rolling effect.

Score
To compress or crease paper to facilitate folding or tearing, to prevent cracking, and to ensure proper placement of the fold.

Self-mailer
A folded piece that is intended to go through the mail system without the protection of an envelope. Self-mailers are subject to the rules and regulations of the postal service.

Sheet
A piece of unfolded paper.

Signature
A folded, printed sheet that forms a section of a printed piece or book. Paging for a signature is usually a multiple of four or eight.

Soft fold
An additional gentle fold in half made by machine, generally for mailing purposes.

Substrate
Any base material with a surface that can be printed or coated.

Text paper
A general term for paper suitable for two-sided printing with a basis size of 25 x 38in (635 x 965.2mm).

Trim
The excess area of a printed form or page in which instructions, register marks, and quality control devices are printed. The trim is cut off before binding.

Wafer seal
Also commonly called a tab, an adhesive seal used to keep a folded piece from opening. Used to meet mailing regulations or for decorative effect.

Waste
The leftover trimmings accumulated when paper is cut after the printing process.

With the grain
Parallel to the grain direction of the paper.

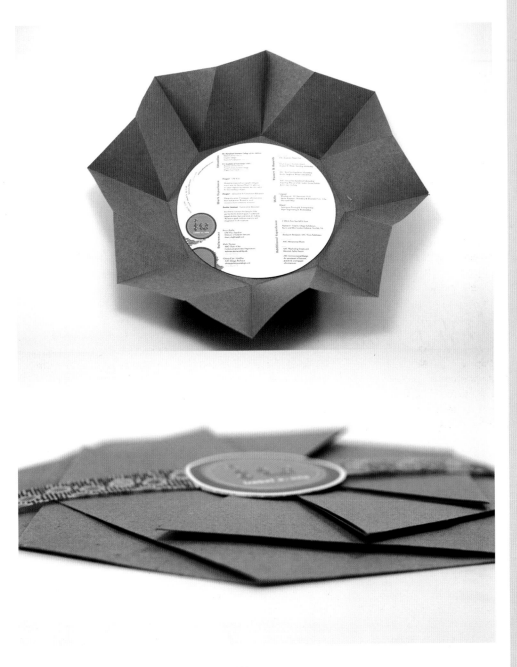

Tato fold resume designed and produced by Isabel Uria

INDEX

ACKNOWLEDGMENTS

I would like to thank all who helped to make this book possible, especially Jason Edwards and Perry Harvey, who worked closely with me on the photography and the templates. Special thanks to all who gave their permission to share photographs of their work in this publication. I am truly grateful to everyone who sends real-world folded materials to foldfactory.com so that we can share them across different forms of media. I look forward to learning more, sharing more, and inspiring everyone to leverage the powerful medium of print.

Thank you Janice Reese, KG and, of course, MXW and the monsters for continued support.